Aspen Health Law Center Current Issues

HEALTH CARE
FRAUD AND ABUSE

Aspen Health Law Center

Aspen Health Law Center Current Issues

Managed Care: State Regulation

Health Care Fraud and Abuse

Physicians as Employees

Employment Discrimination in
the Health Care Industry

Employee Benefits:
A Guide for Health Care Professionals

Aspen Health Law Center Current Issues

HEALTH CARE FRAUD AND ABUSE

Aspen Health Law Center

AN ASPEN PUBLICATION®
Aspen Publishers, Inc.
Gaithersburg, Maryland
1998

This publication is designed to provide accurate and authoritative information in regard to the Subject Matter covered. It is sold with the understanding that the publisher is not engaged in rendering legal, accounting, or other professional service. If legal advice or other expert assistance is required, the service of a competent professional should be sought. (From a Declaration of Principles jointly adopted by a Committee of the American Bar Association and a Committee of Publishers and Associations.)

Library of Congress Cataloging-in-Publication Data
Health care fraud and abuse / Aspen Health Law Center.
p.   cm. — (Aspen Health Law Center current issues)
Includes bibliographical references and index.
ISBN 0-8342-1159-9 (pbk.)
1. Insurance, Health—Law and legislation—United States—Criminal provisions.
2. Medical Care—Law and legislation—United States—Criminal provisions.
3. Medicare fraud.   4. Medicaid fraud.   I. Aspen Health Law Center.   II. Series.
KF3605.H425   1998
345.73'0263—dc21
98-9393
CIP

Orders: (800) 638-8437
Customer Service: (800) 234-1660

About Aspen Publishers • For more than 35 years, Aspen has been a leading professional publisher in a variety of disciplines. Aspen's vast information resources are available in both print and electronic formats. We are committed to providing the highest quality information available in the most appropriate format for our customers. Visit Aspen's Internet site for more information resources, directories, articles, and a searchable version of Aspen's full catalog, including the most recent publications: **http://www.aspenpub.com**
Aspen Publishers, Inc. • The hallmark of quality in publishing
Member of the worldwide Wolters Kluwer group.

Editorial Services: Brian MacDonald
Library of Congress Catalog Card Number: 98-9393
ISBN: 0-8342-1159-9

Printed in the United States of America

1   2   3   4   5

Table of Contents

Preface

This book, *Health Care Fraud and Abuse*, is part of a collection of reference products addressing issues of current interest in the field of health care law. These products are designed to provide up-to-date, easy-to-retrieve information on a variety of topics selected on the basis of their relevance to late-breaking developments in the health care industry. The subjects covered in the inaugural group of products include *Managed Care: State Regulation, Physicians as Employees, Employment Discrimination in the Health Care Industry*, and *Employee Benefits: A Guide for Health Care Professionals*. Other topics will be added to this legal reference series as the need arises.

The books are designed to provide practical overviews of the principal legal issues relating to each topic. They are extensively footnoted, and a Table of Contents and Index provide easy access to the information. Most of the products also offer a selection of support documents, including statutory text, model contract language, and administrative rulings and guidance.

The series is compiled by the attorneys and editors on staff at the Health Law Center of Aspen Publishers, who contributed to developing these products through their writing and research efforts. We hope that these products, either separately or as a group, will meet the busy health care professional's ongoing need for information in the rapidly evolving field of health care law.

INTRODUCTION

The subject of health care fraud and abuse has undergone significant growth in the past decade as a result of the expanding reach of both federal and state legislation and stepped-up enforcement efforts on the part of the Department of Health and Human Services (HHS), the Department of Justice (DOJ), and state Medicaid Fraud Control Units. Health care providers have to contend with a growing number of legislative restrictions on how they conduct business and how they structure relationships among themselves. In fiscal year 1997, the federal government increased its funding to the Federal Bureau of Investigation (FBI) by $9 million over the previous year, to allow the agency to target health care fraud under the provisions of the recently enacted Health Care Insurance Portability and Accountability Act (HIPAA).[1] Criminal convictions under health care fraud legislation have increased from 116 in 1992 to 475 in 1996, following the FBI's investigation of 2,200 cases in 1996 compared with 591 investigations in 1992.[2]

The government also has resorted to creative strategies in enforcing some of the more established legislative tools governing health care fraud and abuse. Recently, the DOJ announced its intent to investigate and prosecute providers under the civil False Claims Act (FCA) based on inadequate quality of care allegations, relying on its success in obtaining a settlement in a similar case against a nursing home where patients allegedly were undernourished.[3] The government's use of the civil FCA in this case would appear to be unprecedented, and in conjunction with statements made by DOJ officials, represents a noteworthy expansion of potential liability under this statute.[4] The federal government also has successfully prosecuted violations of the antikickback statute under the civil FCA, arguing that illegal referrals are false claims under the FCA.[5] The extent to which the government has relied on the civil FCA to enforce fraud and abuse prohibitions has prompted the American Hospital Association to call for a six-month moratorium on

Source: Reprinted from *Hospital Law Manual,* pp. 1–80. © 1998, Aspen Publishers, Inc.

1

Health Care Financing Administration (HCFA), Office of Inspector General (OIG), and DOJ false claims actions, to establish voluntary compliance programs and establish clear guidelines to distinguish simple error from genuine fraud.[6]

This chapter provides an analysis of the types of health care provider activities that fall under federal fraud and abuse prohibitions. These prohibitions are largely defined in the Medicare/Medicaid statute and Stark legislation and are enforced under the auspices of these statutes, the civil FCA, as well as an array of other federal laws applicable to fraudulent activities. This chapter also examines the sanctions (criminal, civil, and administrative) that are available to federal enforcement agencies to curb fraud in the health care industry. Finally, because health care providers need to respond to heightened scrutiny in this area by adopting methods of detecting, correcting, and preventing fraud and abuse, this chapter outlines the components of an effective corporate compliance program.

BASIC PROHIBITIONS UNDER FEDERAL FRAUD AND ABUSE LEGISLATION

Very generally, the types of health care provider activities that fall within federal fraud and abuse prohibitions relate to:

- false claims or other fraudulent billing activities
- bribes or kickbacks, including a complex array of discounts, rebates, profit-sharing agreements, or other business arrangements
- illegal referrals, prohibiting physicians from referring patients for health care services to entities in which the physician has a financial interest.

The prohibition against false claims and fraudulent billing specifically prohibits claims for payment under any federal health care program for any item or service provided by a person who:

- has knowingly and willfully made or caused to be made any false statement or representation of a material fact in application for payment, or

- has furnished services or supplies determined to be substantially in excess of those needed or so lacking as to be worthless.[7]

This language prohibits much more than billing for services not rendered. It can include billing for a more expensive covered item than that actually provided, misrepresentation of the patient's condition for billing purposes, claiming costs for nonchargeable services, and so forth. The vast majority of enforcement efforts are directed at fraudulent billing activities, and more recently many of the enforcement initiatives relating to false claims have been initiated under the federal False Claims Act.[8]

The Medicare/Medicaid statute also prohibits specific categories of referral payments, including kickbacks, bribes, or rebates. Indeed, this particular part of the Medicare/Medicaid statute is often referred to as the "antikickback statute." Specifically, 42 U.S.C. § 1320a-7b(b) forbids any knowing and willful conduct involving the solicitation, receipt, offer, or payment of any kind of remuneration in return for referring an individual or for recommending or arranging the purchase, lease, or ordering of an item or service that may be wholly or partially paid for under a federal health care program. The prohibition is intended to curb the corrupting monetary influence on a physician's decision as to where and when to refer patients. This broadly worded prohibition has been in effect since 1972, but has become increasingly relevant in an industry where health care delivery is evolving toward managed care based on agreements between providers.

The Stark law,[9] banning a more specific type of referral between a physician and entities in which the physician has a financial interest, extends the general prohibition on referrals for remuneration in the antikickback statute to self-referrals. The Stark law stems from the same concerns that both patients' interests and cost-containment initiatives are better served if physician referral decisions are isolated from any financial incentives arising from a physician's investment interests in a health care entity. The law prohibits certain referral relationships altogether, and theoretically at least, eliminates the necessity of determining what constitutes a permissible physician relationship for referral purposes. The simplicity of the basic self-referral ban contained in the Stark legislation is misleading, however, because the numerous statutory exceptions to the ban and its overlap with the antikickback prohibition add significant complications to the statutory scheme.

The HIPAA[10] establishes a series of new criminal offenses relating to health care fraud. A significant section of the statute creates a new federal offense for "health care fraud." The offense of "health care fraud" is defined as "knowingly and willfully executing, or attempting to execute, a scheme or artifice to defraud any health care benefit program or to obtain, by means of false or fraudulent pretenses, representations or promises, any of the money owned by, or under the custody or control of, any health care benefit program." Other federal offenses relating to health care fraud created under the new statute include theft or embezzlement, false statements, and obstruction of criminal investigations.

Fraud and Abuse Prohibitions Relating to False Claims and Fraudulent Billing

As is mentioned in the introduction to this chapter, false claims and fraudulent billing practices are the object of the vast majority of government enforcement initiatives. Very generally, fraud with respect to claims for medical services occurs when the provider in some way misrepresents the nature of the services provided. The specific examples of fraudulent billing practices vary depending on whether the health care provider is operating in a fee-for-service or a capitated environment, because the economic incentives to commit fraud differ depending on the method of reimbursement. In a fee-for-service setting, the economic incentives encourage health care providers to bill for services that were not rendered, to bill for a more expensive service than what was rendered, or to overutilize services by providing unnecessary medical treatment. In a capitated environment, where the health care provider bears the financial risk of providing all covered services to a defined group of beneficiaries, the economic incentives encourage health care providers to obtain a higher capitated rate by submitting false cost data, failing to provide necessary medical services, and enrolling fictitious patients in the plan. The following sections discuss the more common fraudulent billing practices in health care settings that can generate liability for criminal, civil, and/or administrative penalties under federal law.

Claims for Services Not Rendered

Misrepresentations regarding the nature of services provided can take various forms, depending on the type of information that is misrepresented. The misrepresentation can involve a claim for services that were not provided, in some instances simply because no treatment was provided. From an evidence standpoint, this type of practice can be difficult to prove because medical services frequently leave no tangible evidence of their delivery and are often so routine that patients cannot recall if they received the service or not. In addition, some patients are too ill at the time of examination to accurately remember events and provide credible testimony. Health care providers have been successfully prosecuted for billing for services they never provided, however, in cases where delivery of a service can be corroborated by a related event. One such case involved a pharmacist who billed for durable medical equipment (DME), the sale of which requires patients to be fitted. Because the patients in this case testified that they had never been fitted for the equipment, there was sufficient evidence that the equipment had not been provided.[11] Other cases where health care providers have been successfully charged with fraud involve claims for procedures that are so invasive that patients can clearly remember whether or not they underwent the procedure. One such case involved physicians' claims for laryngoscopies, a procedure requiring the insertion of an instrument down a patient's throat, that according to patient testimony were never performed.[12]

Billing for services that were not actually rendered more often than not occurs when some form of service is in fact provided but is not compensable or is compensable at a lower rate under the patient's insurance plan. In these cases, the provider submits a claim for a service that does not correspond to the actual treatment delivered to the patient. This practice, known as "upcoding," has been specifically added to the list of practices that generate liability for civil monetary penalties in the HIPAA.[13] A physician who submits a claim for an office visit when in fact he or she had only telephone contact with a patient, a claim for an allergy shot that was allegedly administered by a physician when in fact a nurse performed the injection, or a claim for an oral cancer consult when in fact the dentist performed only a routine dental screening are examples of this type of misrepresentation. In cases where some service was in fact provided, but misrepresented for billing purposes, fraud is sometimes difficult to prove, however. This can occur because, from the patient's perspective, the services provided closely resemble the ones described on the claim, because the medical record does not contain an accurate record of what service was in fact performed, or because the billing codes for the different services are hard to distinguish.

Providing Medically Unnecessary Services

A false claim also can involve billing for unnecessary services, when submission of the claim requires certification that the service was medically necessary. The HCFA 1500 claim form, for example, requires a physician to certify that the services shown on the form were medically indicated and necessary for the health of the patient. The incentive to perform and bill for unnecessary medical services is present in a fee-for-service environment, but generally would not exist if the services were capitated. The emphasis on volume of services is also the incentive for referral kickbacks, another form of conduct prohibited under the Medicare/Medicaid statute. [For a more detailed discussion of health care fraud and abuse under the antikickback statute, see Fraud and Abuse Prohibitions Relating to Kickbacks and Illegal Remuneration.]

DRG Creep

A practice similar to upcoding that occurs in a hospital setting is known as "DRG creep." Diagnostic-related groups (DRGs) are an example of capitated reimbursement, establishing a prospective payment system (PPS) that defines in advance how much a hospital will receive to provide inpatient services to a specific class of patients. The PPS governing Medicare Part A inpatient hospital services classifies each patient's case into DRGs. The DRG is part of a classification that divides possible diagnoses into more than 20 major body systems and subdivides them into more than 450 groups. The rate attached to each DRG and the corresponding payment for a particular admission are based on a method that assesses the principal and any secondary diagnoses, procedures performed (such as surgery), complications, and other factors. Other factors affecting the DRG rate include size of the community in which the hospital is located, the indirect costs of medical education, and the percentage of low-income patients served by the hospital.

The placement of a patient into a higher-paying category results in the hospital receiving more money for the admission. Over time, patients may be classified into higher-value DRGs than are truly warranted. This can occur, for example, if hospital personnel switch the primary and secondary diagnoses. Likewise, a relatively minor condition might be erroneously assessed as a "complication" (i.e., a condition that arises during the admission and increases the length of stay by at least one day in 75 percent of cases), thus placing the patient into a higher-paying category. DRG creep also can result from computer-based programs or consultant-assisted coding, when the symptoms are common to several diagnoses. This practice of misrepresenting the appropriate DRG and allowing a particular patient to "creep" into a higher-weighted DRG can constitute a false claim under federal health care fraud and abuse prohibitions, especially in light of the OIG's often repeated position that "maximizing reimbursement" is fraudulent.

Fragmenting or "Unbundling" Services

"Unbundling" a claim involves submitting bills separately for procedures when in fact the procedures should be billed as a whole. The practice of unbundling has been at the forefront of recent government enforcement efforts with respect to tests performed by hospital laboratories. For example, a joint HHS OIG and DOJ initiative, launched in Ohio and known as the Lab Unbundling Project, is based on allegations that hospitals violated the FCA when they unbundled outpatient Medicare and Medicaid laboratory test claims by billing them under two or more Physician's Current Procedural Terminology (CPT) codes instead of as a package. Hospital-based laboratories are required to bill for multiple tests performed simultaneously on a patient at a lower rate than the individual tests. In response to charges that they had submitted false claims by billing for tests at the higher individual rate, the hospitals contended that they were never instructed to bundle claims for urinalysis, hematology, and organ disease panel tests.[14]

Fragmenting a claim occurs if a provider submits a claim for separate services when a global billing code is provided. For example, Medicare pays for certain surgical services under global billing codes intended to cover not only the procedure itself, but also the usual pre- and postoperative services. Examples of such improper practices would include billing separately for a biopsy performed as part of a surgical procedure, or billing separately for follow-up visits that occurred within a specified time after the operation. There are exceptions to these rules, however, in cases where, for example, the visits do not relate to the condition leading to surgery or to the postsurgical care.

DRG Payment Window Violations

The recent focus on DRG payment window violations illustrates just how subtle and dangerous payment issues can become. Prior to the PPS, Medicare Part A would pay for hospital outpatient services furnished within 24 hours of an inpatient admission at the same hospital. This served as a benefit to the patient, because it eliminated the 20 percent coinsurance on what otherwise would have been covered under Medicare Part B. When PPS rates were established, HCFA continued the policy of including in the payment for admission those outpatient services performed within 24 hours of admission. However, even after the inception of PPS, the "24-hour DRG payment window" existed only in administrative manuals and was not formally regulated until 1990.

In 1990, Congress expanded the DRG payment window in two ways.[15] First, the time period was expanded from the day prior to the day of admission to three days prior to the day of admission. Moreover, the services falling within the ambit of the law were expanded to include not only hospital outpatient services, but also services furnished by any entity "wholly owned or operated" by a hospital. Therefore, this rule prohibited payment separate from the inpatient hospital reimbursement for covered services, such as diagnostic tests, provided by entities wholly owned and operated by the hospital during the three days preceding the date of admission to the hospital.[16] The phrase "wholly owned or operated" has been interpreted by HCFA as including management agreements whereby hospitals contract with unrelated organizations to manage a clinic. The effective date for this change was retroactive to January 1, 1991, for diagnostic services related to admission and October 1, 1991, for all other services.

Illustrating their intent to rely on the provisions of the civil FCA to extract settlements from health care providers in cases of systemic billing errors, the DOJ and HCFA launched a broad investigation into possible improper billings under the DRG window rule at thousands of hospitals. To this end, DOJ sent letters to target hospitals offering to settle allegedly impermissible claims for outpatient services provided to Medicare beneficiaries within 72 hours of a subsequent inpatient admission. The civil settlements that ensued as a result of this effort clearly demonstrate the power that the government wields against health care providers in such situations, who frequently settle claims with no admission of wrongdoing simply to avoid the financial ruin that would result from a large damage award or exclusion from the Medicare program.

Waiver of Coinsurance and Deductibles

Medicare Parts A and B both contain provisions for copayments and deductibles in connection with services provided.[17] Except in cases where it is determined that a patient is indigent, a provider is not permitted to waive copayments and deductibles, because when such payments are waived, the actual charge becomes lower than the charge that is billed. The government's position is that it is being defrauded, because it is induced to pay the full actual charge, rather than the charge minus the copayment and deductible. As the HHS OIG illustrated in a Special Fraud Alert:

> A provider, practitioner, or supplier who routinely waives co-payments or deductibles is misstating its actual charge. For example, if a supplier claims that its charge for a piece of equipment is $100, but routinely waives the co-payment, the actual charge is $80. Medicare should be paying 80% of $80 (or $64), rather than 80% of $100 (or $80). As a result of the supplier's misrepresentation, the Medicare program is paying $16 more than it should for this item.[18]

The HIPAA[19] specifies that civil monetary penalties can be imposed for offering remuneration to individuals who are eligible for Medicare and Medicaid benefits if the person making the offer knows or should know that the remuneration will influence the patient to order or receive items or services from a particular provider. The statutory definition of "remuneration" includes the waiver of coinsurance and deductible amounts, but specifies that a waiver of coinsurance and deductibles is possible under certain circumstances. The term "remuneration" does not include:

- the waiver of coinsurance and deductible amounts if the waiver is not offered as part of any advertisement or solicitation, the person does not routinely waive coinsurance or deductible amounts, and the person either does not collect after making a reasonable effort to collect or after a good-faith determination that the patient is in financial need;
- differentials in coinsurance and deductible amounts as part of a benefit plan design as long as the differentials have been disclosed to beneficiaries, third-party payers, and providers and meet standards established by the Secretary; or
- incentives given to individuals to promote the delivery of preventive care but only as determined by the Secretary in regulations.

It is important to note that, unlike the antikickback statute, no intent to induce referrals or orders for services is necessary for liability to arise under these circumstances, as long as the government can demonstrate that the person offering the remuneration should have known that the action would influence the patient's selection of a health care provider. The text of the Conference Report on the HIPAA indicates that this provision does not prohibit offering items and services of nominal value, such as refreshments, medical literature, free local transportation, or health fairs.[20]

False Cost Reports

Health care facilities, such as hospitals, nursing homes, and home health agencies, also can generate false claims liability by submitting cost reports to health care programs that contain false or fraudulent information. Cost reports must be submitted annually to be eligible for reimbursement under Medicare and Medicaid. The amount due to these providers is calculated by a formula that incorporates the actual cost of delivering health care services to patients. With respect to these cost reports, fraud occurs when the information provided adds costs that are unrelated to patient care, inflates actual patient care costs, or fails to reveal that the provider is dealing with related organizations. Errors that can lead to charges of fraudulent conduct include: incorrect apportionment of costs, inclusion of noncovered services or equipment in allowable costs, claims for bad debts without a genuine attempt to collect payment, depreciation of assets that have already been fully depreciated or sold, and statistic manipulation to obtain additional payment.[21]

Payments To Induce Reduction or Limitation of Services

Physician incentive programs (PIPs) are programs that reward or penalize physicians depending on whether they deliver health care services within the utilization parameters established by the health care organization. With the implementation of a PPS, some hospitals adopted PIPs that offered physicians incentives to control the length of stay of Medicare beneficiaries. Effective with payments on or after April 21, 1987, hospitals are prohibited from making any direct or indirect payment to a physician as an inducement to limit services to patients under the physician's direct care who are entitled to Medicare or Medicaid benefits.[22] The hospital that knowingly makes such a payment, as well as any physician who knowingly accepts it, is subject to a civil monetary penalty of up to $2,000 for each patient for whom payment is made.

In a proposed rule to implement the imposition of civil monetary penalties under this provision, the OIG has recommended that hospitals adopt certain measures with respect to PIPs, including: basing plan payments on the cost performance of a group of physicians rather than on the performance of an individual physician, evaluating performance over a relatively long period of time (one year as opposed to monthly or quarterly), and not basing incentive payments on the hospital's treatment of any individual patient.[23]

False Claims Liability for Managed Care Organizations

The advent of managed care has added some new wrinkles to the subject of false claims and fraudulent billing. When payments to providers are capitated, with a fixed per-patient amount, there is no financial incentive to order unnecessary treatment, as there is in a fee-for-service environment. Rather, with capitation, the incentives run the other way, toward underutilization, because the provider generally receives the same amount regardless of the level of treatment. Thus, a false claim is more likely to take the form of denial of services rather than billing for unnecessary services. For example, a managed care plan may offer a certain number of free office visits or other services to members, but a physician may discourage such visits, telling patients they are unnecessary. Plan employees may also misrepresent the availability of services to beneficiaries to discourage their use. Accepting a capitated payment while denying agreed-to services would constitute a false claim, although perhaps in a more subtle form than a traditional false claim.

Another way that services can be denied to managed care plan members is to screen out those members of an eligible group who appears to be less healthy, and to encourage them to go back to the traditional Medicare program. In this way, a healthier pool of patients who require fewer services can be diverted into the managed care plan.

A managed care organization (MCO) that applies for a Medicare risk contract must provide certain information to HCFA, demonstrating that it has the ability to enroll members and to deliver a specified comprehensive range of high-quality services efficiently, effectively, and economically to Medicare enrollees. MCOs therefore are exposed to potential liability for fraud if the information contained in the application is misrepresented. In addition, civil monetary penalties may be assessed if these organizations engage in specific activities.[24] These activities include: exceeding permitted premiums, misrepresenting or falsifying information presented to the Medicare program, preventing or discouraging the enrollment of individuals with medical histories that would indicate a substantial future need for medical services, illegally expelling or refusing to re-enroll a beneficiary, and failing to comply with provisions regarding the operation of a PIP. With respect to this latter activity, HCFA has published final regulations governing PIPs offered by federally qualified HMOs and competitive medical plans (CMPs) that contract with the Medicare program and certain HMOs and health insuring organizations that contract with the Medicaid program.[25] These regulations specify that an organization can operate a PIP if there is no specific payment made directly or indirectly to a physician or physician group as an inducement to reduce or limit medically necessary services furnished to Medicare or Medicaid. Finally, the HIPAA[26] further allows civil monetary penalties (intermediate sanctions) to be imposed on HMOs and CMPs with Medicare contracts for failing to substantially carry out the contract in a manner substantially inconsistent with the efficient and effective administration of the Social Security Act[27] or for being out of substantial compliance with certain provisions of the Act.

Fraud and Abuse Prohibitions Relating to Kickbacks and Illegal Remuneration

Soliciting, offering, or receiving any payment (including but not limited to a kickback, bribe, or rebate) in return for the opportunity to do business or the referral of patients for services reimbursable under Medicare or Medicaid is illegal.

Specifically, Section 1320a-7b in the Medicare/Medicaid anti-kickback statute provides that:

(1) Whoever knowingly and willfully solicits or receives any remuneration (including any kickback, bribe or rebate) directly or indirectly, overtly or covertly, in cash or in kind

(A) in return for referring an individual to a person for the furnishing or arranging for the furnishing of any item or service for which payment may be made in whole or in part under a Federal health care program, or

(B) in return for purchasing, leasing or ordering, or arranging for or recommending purchasing, leasing or ordering any good, facility, service or item for which payment may be made in whole or in part under a Federal health care program, shall be guilty of a felony and upon conviction thereof, shall be fined not more than $25,000 or imprisoned for not more than five years or both.

(2) Whoever knowingly and willfully offers or pays any remuneration (including kickback, bribe or rebate) directly or indirectly, overtly or covertly, in cash or in kind to any person to induce such person

(A) to refer an individual to a person for the furnishing or arranging for the furnishing of any item or service for which payment may be made in whole or in part under a Federal health care program, or

(B) to purchase, lease, order or arrange for or recommend purchasing, leasing or ordering any good, facility, service or item for which payment may be made in whole or in part under a Federal health care program, shall be guilty of a felony and upon conviction thereof, shall be fined not more than $25,000 or imprisoned for not more than five years or both.[28]

This broadly worded prohibition is principally intended to restrict the corrupting influence of money on a physician's decision as to when and where to refer patients. Any arrangement that ties payment to patient referrals, directly or indirectly, is potentially troublesome under this law, so prudence dictates that experienced Medicare counsel be consulted in implementing any such venture.

For example, the question of referral payments may arise in hospitals' joint ventures with members of their medical staffs, with physician recruitment inducements, in group purchasing, or in contracts with purveyors of specialized goods or services such as durable medical equipment, respiratory therapy, or cardiac monitoring.

"Remuneration" is broadly defined to include any payment in cash or in kind, made either directly or indirectly, overtly or covertly. Remuneration does not include, however, a discount or price reduction if the amount is properly disclosed and reflected in the cost claimed as reimbursement or in charges. Remuneration also does not include any amount paid by an employer to an employee for work performed in providing covered items for services. Both HCFA and the OIG have indicated that the term "remuneration" refers to any economic benefit, which can be conferred in a variety of ways, including reduced rent, compensation guarantees, equipment loans, administrative and billing services, and participation in ventures offering the opportunity to generate fees.

In 1985, the Third Circuit examined the issue of whether payments to a physician were a kickback for patient referrals or could be justified by services rendered. In *United States v. Greber*,[29] the appeals court upheld the criminal conviction of a physician who had paid other physicians "interpretation fees" for each patient referred to a cardiac monitoring service. The payment in question was 40 percent of the amount the physician's company received from Medicare, not to exceed $65 per patient.

The evidence showed that the interpretation fees were paid for the physicians' initial consultation services, as well as for explaining test results to patients. However, there also was evidence that the physicians received the fees even when the physician interpreted the data, that the amount paid was more than Medicare would allow for such services, and that the defendant had testified that without the fee, physicians would not use his service. In upholding the conviction, the court adopted a broad interpretation of the antikickback statute:

> The text [of the law] refers to "any remuneration."
> That includes not only sums for which no actual ser-
> vice was performed but also those amounts for which
> some professional time was expended. "Remunerates"
> is defined as "to pay an equivalent for service." . . .
> That a particular payment was a remuneration (which
> implies that a service was rendered) rather than a kick-
> back does not foreclose the possibility that a violation
> nevertheless could exist.
>
> . . .
>
> We conclude that the more expansive reading is
> consistent with the impetus for the 1977 amend-
> ments. . . . If the payments were intended to induce
> the physicians to use Cardio-Med's services, the statute
> was violated, even if the payments were also intended
> to compensate for professional services.[30]

The *Greber* holding that the anitkickback law is violated if one
purpose (as opposed to the sole purpose) of the payment is to
induce referrals was adopted by the Ninth Circuit in *United
States v. Kats*[31] and the First Circuit in *United States v. Bay State
Ambulance & Hospital Rental Service.*[32]

As it is drafted, the antikickback statute makes illegal numerous common business practices that are completely unrelated
to bribes or kickbacks. For example, a pharmacy's rental of
space in an office building that is owned by the physician occu-
pants of the building could generate antikickback concerns if
the pharmacy pays the physician landlords a base rent plus a
percentage of gross revenue. This type of arrangement may be a
traditional commercial lease arrangement for a retail establishment, but it could be argued that the percentage of gross revenues are illegal kickbacks to the physician owners of the building in exchange for their referral of Medicare and Medicaid
patients to the pharmacy.

Hospital/Physician Joint Ventures

Although the antikickback prohibition has been on the books
since 1972, the proliferation of health care joint ventures in the

1980s prompted HHS to focus more closely on the issue of physician self-referral. In particular, the OIG has expressed concern that joint venture arrangements are created primarily as vehicles to induce physicians to refer patients and enhance revenues, rather than as a means to provide new needed services.

In 1989, the OIG issued a Special Fraud Alert on the subject of Joint Venture Arrangements, in an attempt to publicly describe suspect features of joint ventures and to encourage providers to independently disband many of these arrangements.[33] According to the Fraud Alert, the OIG will consider an arrangement to be a "suspect joint venture" if investors are potential referral sources; if physicians who are likely to be significant referral sources are provided the opportunity to purchase a larger share in the entity; if physicians are encouraged to refer to the entity or divest interest when referrals fall below an "acceptable" level; if the entity tracks and distributes information regarding referral sources; if physicians are required to divest interest upon retirement or any other change in status that makes them unable to refer; or if an investment interest is nontransferable.

In 1989, the OIG brought its first action to administratively impose exclusions from the Medicare and Medicaid programs in a case that involved three joint venture, limited partnership clinical laboratories in different California locations. In *Inspector General v. Hanlester Network*[34] an administrative law judge (ALJ) held that all of the participants in a clinical laboratory joint venture violated the Medicare antikickback law; the Ninth Circuit upheld the finding of liability as to all but five individual investors in the joint venture. The Board had concluded that the ALJ should have excluded all of the participants from the Medicare program. The ALJ had permanently excluded some of the participants, and had imposed two-year exclusions on others. He had refused to exclude five individuals, however, finding that they are unlikely to engage in future illegal conduct and that no remedial purpose would be served by exclusion.

The Board reversed the decision not to exclude the remaining participants. In deciding whether to impose exclusion, the ALJ incorrectly focused on whether a party manifests any propensity to engage in illegal or harmful conduct, the Board explained, which put the burden on the Inspector General to prove untrustworthiness. Instead, an inference of untrustworthiness arises from the individual's illegal acts, and the burden is on them to come forward with evidence to overcome the inference arising from their illegal behavior. In this case, the Board found that the participants did not do that. The Board also ruled that the uncertain state of the law as to whether the activity was illegal when it occurred did not absolve the participants of culpability, and had no bearing on their future trustworthiness in complying with the law.

The Ninth Circuit subsequently refused to uphold HHS's decision to exclude participants in the Hanlester joint venture from the Medicare/Medicaid program, although its ruling partially endorses HHS's interpretation of the antikickback statute in this case. The court agreed with HHS that the statute was not void for vagueness and that evidence of a formal agreement to refer program-related business is not necessary to establish a violation of the antikickback statute. A violation of the statute can occur when an individual or entity knowingly and willfully offers or pays any remuneration, in any manner or form, to induce the referral of program-related business. The court found, however, that there was insufficient evidence that the parties offered or paid remuneration to induce referrals. Payments were made to the physician limited partners based on each individual's ownership share of profits and not on the volume of their referrals, whether or not they referred business to the joint venture laboratories. The fact that a large number of referrals resulted in the potential for a high return on investment or that the practical effect of low referral rates would result in failure for the laboratories was insufficient to prove that the parties offered or paid remuneration to induce referrals, the court declared. The partnership's marketing director's representations to the limited partners did constitute offers of payments to induce program-related business, however, and the network and joint venture laboratories were vicariously liable for her violation of the statute. Because the liability of these parties was strictly vicarious, any untrustworthiness on their part disappeared when the employment relationship with the marketing director ended. Accordingly, the court concluded, their exclusion from the Medicare/Medicaid program is unnecessary.[35]

Hospital/Physician Recruitment and Retention

In the early 1990s, the OIG began directing its enforcement efforts under the antikickback statute to situations where physicians received referrals from hospitals. In its 1991 Management Advisory Report (MAR) entitled *Financial Arrangements between Hospitals and Hospital-based Physicians*,[36] the OIG states that arrangements between hospitals and hospital-based physicians can violate the statute if they require physicians to pay more than fair market value for services provided by the hospitals.

According to the MAR, hospitals are in a position where they can direct referrals to hospital-based physicians, defined to include anesthesiologists, pathologists, and radiologists. The antikickback statute would be implicated in such referrals if hospital-based physicians pay for these services through the Medicare and Medicaid programs. Suspect agreements include those that require physicians to pay more than fair market value for services provided by the hospitals and that compensate physicians for less than the fair market value of the goods and services they provide to hospitals. The MAR recommends that contracts between hospitals and hospital-based physicians be based on the fair market value of services, unrelated to physician billings and limited to goods and services necessary for the provision of medical services by the hospital-based physicians.

In 1992, the OIG continued to focus on hospital/physician relationships, issuing a Special Fraud Alert on the subject of hospital recruitment and retention programs that are intended, at least in part, to influence a physician's hospital referral decisions.[37] According to the Special Fraud Alert, "suspect incentive arrangements" include payment of an incentive for each referral; free or significantly discounted office space, equipment, or staff services; compensation guarantees; low-interest or interest-free loans that are subject to forgiveness based on referral patterns; payment of a physician's travel expenses or continuing education courses; inappropriately low-cost coverage on a hospital's insurance plans; and payment for services that exceed their fair market value. The Special Fraud Alert reiterates the OIG's position that the antikickback statute is violated if a hospital provides a benefit to a physician with the intent of inducing referrals from the physician to the hospital, unless the arrangement falls within one of the existing safe harbors. [For a more extensive discussion of the safe harbors under the antikickback statute, see The Safe Harbor Regulations.]

Reflecting the OIG's view on this type of arrangement, a federal trial court in Texas recently struck down a physician-hospital agreement under the antikickback statute.[38] Under a recruitment agreement with a physician, a hospital was obligated to provide the physician with an office for three months at no cost, to provide a capped amount of free utilities for the physician's office, and to reimburse the physician's moving expenses and malpractice insurance premiums for the first year. The court found that the hospital had in effect provided the physician with remuneration in the form of an interest-free loan, as well as free office space, rent, utilities, subsidies, and reimbursement for medical malpractice insurance. Because the remunerations were clearly subject to the physician's referral of patients to the hospital and therefore violated the antikickback statute, the court refused to enforce the agreement.[39]

Hospital Purchases of Physician Practices

In response to health care reform initiatives, many hospitals are extending their operations into managed care arrangements and integrated delivery systems. This process has frequently involved the acquisition of physician group practices by hospitals. The OIG has expressed concern regarding these types of acquisitions, however, because the payments to the selling physicians can constitute illegal remuneration for patient referrals.

The OIG spelled out its concerns in a December 22, 1992, letter sent to the Office of the Associate Chief Counsel at the Internal Revenue Service (IRS).[40] The IRS informally requested the HHS's views regarding the application of the antikickback statute to hospital purchases of physician practices where the physician seller continues to treat patients and is affiliated with the purchasing hospital. In its letter, the OIG stated that hospitals seek to purchase physician practices as a means to attract new referrals. The remuneration paid for the practice can constitute the "illegal remuneration to induce the referral of business reimbursed by the Medicare or Medicaid programs. . . . The same concerns arise where another entity (such as a foundation) purchases a physician practice, when such foundation also owns or operates a hospital which benefits from referrals from those physicians." The OIG expressed fear that the remuneration paid in conjunction with the acquisition of a physician practice could interfere with the physician's subsequent judgment regarding appropriate care for a patient, inflate costs to the Medicare and Medicaid programs, and interfere with a beneficiary's freedom of choice of providers.

According to the OIG letter, two issues are crucial to determining if a physician practice acquisition violates the antikickback statute. The first issue concerns the amount of compensation paid to the physician and the types of items for which the physician receives payment. Any amount paid for assets that relate to the continuing treatment of the physician's patients could be considered as payment for referrals, the letter said, because those assets have value only in the context of continued treatment of the physician's patients. In particular, payment for good will, noncompete covenants, exclusive dealing agreements, patient lists, and patient records would be open to question. Accordingly, the OIG suggests, it may be necessary to exclude these intangibles from the fair market value assessment of a physician practice for the purposes of antikickback analysis. This position conflicts with the IRS's acceptance of a valuation method that includes the value of tangible as well as intangible assets, prompting the IRS to insert a caveat in a private letter ruling granting tax-exempt status to an integrated delivery system formed in part through the purchase of a physician practice.[41]

The second issue involves the amount and manner in which the physician is subsequently compensated for providing services to the hospital. The letter queries the legitimacy of subsequent payments to physicians even if they are hospital employees. Although the statute exempts any amount paid by an employer to an employee who has a bona fide employment relationship with the employer in the provision of covered items or services, the letter implies that this exemption does not permit a hospital to pay a physician employee for patient referrals. The OIG states in this regard that "since referrals do not represent covered items or services, payments to employees, which are for the purpose of compensating such employees for the referral of patients, would likely not be covered by the employee exemption."

Fraud Alerts, Advisory Opinions, and Other Administrative Guidance

As is illustrated in the preceding sections, the OIG often issues Fraud Alerts on the subject of arrangements that might violate the antikickback statute. These Fraud Alerts provide health care providers with useful guidance on how to structure payment and other financial relationships. In addition to the Fraud Alerts relating to joint venture arrangements and hospital incentives to physicians, for example, other Fraud Alerts issued by the OIG have focused on the routine waiver of copayments or deductibles under Medicare Part B [for a more detailed discussion of this topic, see Waiver of Coinsurance and Deductibles] prescription drug marketing schemes, clinical laboratory services, and home health fraud.

In addition, and of significant importance to health care providers, is a new statutory requirement under the HIPAA[42] that the Secretary of HHS issue advisory opinions on designated matters to individuals or entities who apply for them. The statute lists the matters on which HHS is required to issue opinions, including what constitutes prohibited remuneration under the antikickback statute, whether an arrangement falls within a statutory exception or safe harbor under the antikickback statute, and whether a specific activity constitutes grounds for sanctions under the antikickback statute. The statute specifically states, however, that certain matters are not subject to advisory opinions; what constitutes "fair market value" within a particular transaction and whether an individual is a bona fide employee for the purposes of Section 3121(D)(2) of the Internal Revenue Code cannot be the subject of an advisory opinion.[43]

THE SAFE HARBOR REGULATIONS[44]

Under the Medicare/Medicaid statute, HHS is authorized to issue regulations specifying payment practices that will not be subject to criminal prosecution or provide a basis for exclusion under the antikickback statute.[45] The OIG finalized 11 safe harbor regulations in 1991,[46] and added additional managed care safe harbors in 1992.[47] In 1993, the OIG proposed 7 additional safe harbors,[48] and proposed a rule clarifying the safe harbors in 1994.[49] In addition, under the HIPAA,[50] the Secretary of HHS is required to solicit proposals either to amend existing safe harbors or to create new ones. In this regard, the statute enumerates eight criteria that may be considered by the OIG in regulating safe harbors. Seven of the criteria involve increases or decreases in access to health care services; quality of health care services; competition among health care providers; patients' freedom of choice among providers; the ability of health care facilities to provide services in medically underserved areas or to medically underserved populations; the cost to federal health care programs; and the potential overutilization of health care service. The eighth criterion that the OIG may consider is the existence of any potential financial benefit to a health care professional or provider that may be affected by the decision of whether to order a health care item or service or to arrange for a referral to a particular practitioner or provider.

A health care provider must comply fully with the conduct defined in the safe harbors to obtain protection against civil or criminal prosecution, although good-faith efforts to comply with the regulations will be relevant to determining whether prosecution is warranted.[51] The following sections discuss the safe harbors that are currently in effect.

Investment Interests in Large Publicly Traded Entities and Small Ventures

The investment interests safe harbors are intended to allow practitioners to invest in medical facilities in situations where the financial incentives to refer to those facilities have been contained. Liability under the antikickback statute can arise when a practitioner invests in a facility to which he or she refers patients, if the return on the investment is linked to those referrals. The investment interests safe harbors recognize that a provider may legitimately invest in a medical facility, however, and allow investment in both large and small ventures under specific conditions.

The regulations define an "investment interest" in an entity as a security issued by the entity. It may include the following classes of investments:

- shares in a corporation
- interests or units of a partnership
- bonds, debentures, notes, or other debt instruments

An "investor" is defined as an individual or entity who either:

- holds a direct investment interest in an entity, or
- holds such investment interest indirectly by means such as:
  - having a family member hold such investment interest, or
  - holding a legal or beneficial interest in another entity (such as a trust or holding company) that holds such investment interest

The OIG has stated expressly that these examples of indirect investment interests are intended to be illustrative only, not exhaustive.

With respect to investments in large publicly traded entities, there is no violation inherent in a payment that is a return on an investment interest (such as a dividend or interest income) made to an investor, as long as *all* of the following standards are met:[52]

- The entity must possess, within the previous fiscal year or previous 12-month period, more than $50,000,000 in undepreciated net tangible assets (based on the net acquisition cost of purchasing such assets from an unrelated entity) related to the furnishing of items and services payable under Medicare or Medicaid.
- With respect to an investment interest that is an equity security, the equity security must be registered with the

Securities and Exchange Commission under 15 U.S.C. § 781(b) or (g).

- The investment interest of an investor in a position to make or influence referrals to, furnish items or services to, or otherwise generate business for the entity must be obtained on terms equally available to the public through trading on a registered national securities exchange.
- Neither the entity or any investor may market or furnish entity's items or services to passive investors differently than to noninvestors. This prohibition also applies to items or services furnished by another entity as part of a cross-referral agreement.
- The entity must not loan funds to, or guarantee a loan for, an investor who is in a position to make or influence referrals to, furnish items or services to, or otherwise generate business for the entity if the investor uses any part of such loan to obtain the investment interest.
- Payment to an investor as return on investment must be directly proportional to the amount of that investor's capital investment.

With respect to smaller ventures, there is no violation inherent in a payment that is a return on an investment interest (such as a dividend or interest income) made to an investor, as long as *all* of the following eight standards are met:[53]

1. No more than 40 percent of the value of the investment interests of each class of investments may be held in the previous fiscal year or previous 12-month period by investors who are in a position to make or influence referrals to, furnish items or services to, or otherwise generate business for the entity.
2. Terms on which an investment interest is offered to a passive investor (if any) who is in a position to make or influence referrals to, furnish items or services to, or otherwise generate business for the entity must be no different from the terms offered to other passive investors.
3. Terms on which an investment interest is offered to an investor who is in a position to make or influence referrals

to, furnish items or services to, or otherwise generate business for the entity must not be related to the previous or expected volume of referrals, items or services furnished, or the amount of business otherwise generated from that investor to the entity.

4. The entity has no requirement that a passive investor (if any) make referrals to, be in a position to make or influence referrals to, furnish items or services to, or otherwise generate business for the entity as a condition for remaining as an investor.

5. Neither the entity nor any investor may market or furnish the entity's items or services to passive investors differently than to noninvestors. This prohibition also applies to items or services furnished by another entity as part of a cross-referral agreement.

6. No more than 40 percent of the gross revenue of the entity in the previous fiscal year or previous 12-month period may come from referrals, items or services furnished, or business otherwise generated from investors.

7. The entity must not loan funds to or guarantee a loan for an investor who is in a position to make or influence referrals to, furnish items or services to, or otherwise generate business for the entity if the investor used any part of the loan to obtain the investment interest.

8. Payment to an investor as return on investment must be directly proportional to the amount of that investor's capital investment (including the fair market value of any preoperational services rendered).

This particular safe harbor area fueled much debate and commentary. Note that there is a distinction between investors who are seeking only an investment return, and investors who do business with the entity or who have an ability to do so. (Whether the investor fits in this latter category is a factual question.) The OIG has stated specifically in the preamble to the regulations that his office considers hospitals, as well as physicians, to be capable of influencing referrals.

The preamble gives examples of some very limited situations in which a physician-investor, who otherwise would be categorized as one who is "in a position to make referrals" to an entity, would be found not to be in a position to make referrals, including:

- retired physicians who no longer make or influence referrals
- physicians who reside and practice in a separate service area from the entity
- physician-investors who sign a written agreement stipulating "that for the life of the investment the investor will not make referrals to, furnish items or services for, or otherwise generate business for the entity"

There is a distinction between passive and active investors; some of the standards must be met by both types, while others have to be met by only passive investors. An "active investor" is defined as one who either (1) is responsible for the day-to-day management of the entity and is a bona fide general partner in a partnership under the Uniform Partnership Act or (2) agrees in writing to undertake liability for the actions of the entity's agents acting within the scope of their agency. Every investor who is not an "active investor" under this narrow definition is deemed to be a "passive investor." The term specifically includes limited partners, corporate shareholders, and holders of debt securities.

For an entity with investors to qualify for the small venture safe harbor, all of those investors must meet all the standards imposed on them. The preamble states: "To the extent that one class of investors, such as active investors, qualifies, but the passive investors do not meet one of the standards, safe-harbor protection is not given to payments to any investors in the entity."

The 60 percent–40 percent investment and 60 percent–40 percent referral standards are likely to create the most problems for joint ventures that were established before the publication of the safe harbor regulations. In the preamble, HHS stated that the OIG considers the 60 percent–40 percent investment standard to be a bright-line, outcome-oriented test, and at least 60 percent of the value of the investment interests "must be held by investors who will neither make referrals nor engage in business activity with the entity." It is significant that investors who provide items and services to the entity are treated as equivalent to those who make or influence referrals to the entity.

In classifying the 60 percent–40 percent revenue standard as an additional bright-line rule, the OIG said that this requirement, in conjunction with the 60 percent–40 percent investment interest rule, "will help assure that joint ventures are not dependent on the capital and referrals of physician investors." Section 1001.953 of the Safe Harbor Rules requires the OIG to report to the Secretary on the compliance with these two 60–40 rules within 180 days of the rules' effective date. However, HHS has said that "it is highly unlikely [the OIG] will pursue an investigation of a joint venture where it complies with all the other standards in this safe harbor, is out of compliance with this 60 percent–40 percent standard based on its prior fiscal year data, but is making a good-faith effort to reach compliance with this standard based on data showing compliance on a monthly basis for the most recent months of operation."

In applying the two 60–40 rules, the preamble indicates that where the joint venture entity is owned by other entities, the OIG will examine their ownership structure "to determine whether they are owned by physicians who are referring to the joint venture entity." In other words, investment interests will be traced back through all layers to identify compliance with the 60–40 rules.

Interestingly, the small investment safe harbor does not place any importance on whether or not the existence of investments by those who refer patients to, or do business with, the entity has any effect on the medical necessity of the goods or services the entity provides. The preamble states that utilization review is encouraged, but not required.

The OIG is considering providing additional safe-harbor protection to physician-owned facilities where the physician-owner refers patients to an entity in which the same physician treats the patients. Possible physician-owned facilities to be covered include:

- renal dialysis facilities owned by nephrologists
- ambulatory surgery centers owned by surgeons
- radiation therapy facilities owned by radiation oncologists

Lease of Space and Equipment Rental

These safe harbors are designed to permit legitimate arrangements for the rental of space and equipment, while preventing payments for these commodities that in reality are a subterfuge for kickbacks. The OIG has characterized as two different safe harbors two kinds of lease arrangements: those for space[54] and those for equipment.[55] Despite this characterization, however, the rules for these two safe harbors are very similar; rental payments made by lessees to lessors for use of space or equipment receive safe-harbor protection if *all* of the following five standards are met:

1. The lease agreement is set out in writing and signed by the parties.
2. The lease agreement specifies the premises, equipment, or services to be provided.
3. If the lease agreement is intended to provide for use of premises or equipment on a periodic, sporadic, or part-time basis, rather than a full-time basis for the term of the agreement, the agreement specifies exactly the schedule of such intervals, their precise length, and the exact charge for such intervals.
4. The term of the agreement is for not less than one year.
5. The aggregate compensation paid over the term of the agreement is set in advance, is consistent with fair market value in arm's-length transactions, and is not determined in a manner that takes into account the volume or value of any referrals or business otherwise generated between the parties for which payment may be made in whole or in part under Medicare or a state health program.

A crucial element of both of the lease safe harbors is the regulations' definition of "fair market value." The term is defined to mean:

> The value of the equipment when obtained from a manufacturer or professional distributor, or rental property for general commercial purposes, but *not adjusted to reflect the additional value that either the prospective lessee or the lessor would attribute to the equip-*

ment or property as a result of its proximity or convenience to sources of referrals or business otherwise generated for which payment may be made in whole or in part under Medicare or a State health program.

The preamble also warns of sham contracts in which everything looks good on paper but where there is no intent to have the space or equipment used. (The same warning applies to services provided under the personal service contracts covered below.) The preamble states that although percentage or per-use leases and contracts are not per se violations of the antikickback statute, such arrangements arouse suspicion and need to be examined on a case-by-case basis: "[T]he more the payments appear to reflect the volume of referrals from the financially interested party, the more suspect the arrangement becomes and the more likely [the OIG] will need to examine it carefully."

A lease or contract may contain an early termination clause (including personal service contracts covered below); its legitimacy turns on the parties' intent: "Termination 'for cause' clauses drafted in compliance with the [Internal Revenue Service] IRS or other legal or regulatory requirements should not jeopardize safe-harbor status, if the purpose of the termination clause is to comply with those requirements, and not to facilitate renegotiation for contract terms."

Personal Services and Management Contracts

This safe harbor allows certain service agreements between providers, but prevents the abusive financial situation that arises when the payments for the services exceed fair market value and are linked to referral.[56] For example, this safe harbor could apply to a pediatric cardiologist in private practice who is on staff at a hospital to which he or she also refers patients. As part of an expansion of its pediatric services and facilities, the hospital needs to hire a part-time cardiologist to provide health care services one day per week. To this end, the cardiologist and the hospital enter into a two-year written independent contractor agreement specifying the services the cardiologist will provide one day per week from 9:00 A.M. to 4:00 P.M. for an annual salary of $30,000. As structured, this arrangement fits within the personal services safe harbor as long as the compensation is for fair market value and is not based in any way on referrals from the cardiologist.

Safe harbor protection applies to payments made by a principal to an agent as compensation for the services of the agent, as long as *all* of the following six standards are met:

1. The agency agreement is set out in writing and signed by the parties.
2. The agency agreement specifies the services to be provided by the agent.
3. If the agency agreement is intended to provide for the services of the agent on a periodic, sporadic, or part-time basis, rather than a full-time basis for the term of the agreement, the agreement specifies exactly the schedule of such intervals, their precise length, and the exact charge for such intervals.
4. The term of the agreement is for not less than one year.
5. The aggregate compensation paid to the agent over the term of the agreement is set in advance, is consistent with fair market value in arm's-length transactions, and is not determined in a manner that takes into account the volume or value of any referrals or business otherwise generated between the parties for which payment may be made in whole or in part under Medicare or a state health care program.
6. Services performed under the agreement do not involve the counseling or promotion of a business arrangement or other activity that violates any state or federal law.

Once again, a key definition—not consistent with the common meaning of the term—delineates the scope of this safe harbor. "Agent of a principal" is defined to mean: "Any person other than a bona fide employee of the principal who has an agreement to perform services for, or on behalf of, the principal."

For the first time, the OIG has indicated that salespeople paid on commission may run afoul of the antikickback provisions of the Fraud and Abuse Act. The preamble declares that commission sales arrangements must meet the standards of the safe harbor provisions governing personal services and management contracts to receive protection.

The sixth criterion for the personal-services safe harbor is meant to address consulting and marketing services by making clear "that the service that is contracted for is not protected if it involves the counseling or promotion of a business arrangement or other activity which itself constitutes a violation of any State or Federal law." However, marketing and advertising activities per se are not seen as warranting prosecution (but do warrant safe-harbor protection), even though technically they may violate the antikickback statute. The OIG's reasoning for granting them such protection is that they generally do not involve direct contact with program beneficiaries, or the promoter itself is not involved with health care delivery.

Sale of Practitioner Practice

This safe harbor allows the sale of an ongoing physician practice while curtailing the possibility that the sale price of the practice includes illegal remuneration for referrals.[57] Payments made to a practitioner by another practitioner to purchase a practice are protected as long as the following two standards are met:

1. The period from the date of the first agreement pertaining to the sale to the completion of the sale is not more than one year. [However, the preamble states that this safe harbor does not "preclude a purchaser from making payments to a practitioner beyond the one-year period as long as the other conditions of this provision have been met."]
2. The selling practitioner must not be in a professional position to make referrals to, or otherwise generate business for, the purchasing practitioner for which partial or whole payment may be made under Medicare or a state health program after one year from the date of the first agreement relating to the sale.

These provisions also pertain to option agreements on sales of physicians' practices, as the OIG believes that this is a significant area of abuse. "Often, . . . payments for the sale or option agreement are actually payments for referrals."

Many hospitals purchase physician practices as part of recruitment. The preamble states that although this activity implicates the antikickback statute, the OIG is considering the publication of a separate regulation that may protect many recruitment activities. However, the preamble says that where a hospital purchases a physician's practice "in order to ensure the hospital of a steady stream of referrals," the "very abuses that the statute is designed to prevent" may occur. Accordingly, no safe-harbor protection is afforded to a hospital's purchase of a physician practice—even at fair market value—where the physician is retained on the medical staff.

The preamble also states that there is no safe-harbor protection—despite the "bona fide employee" exception discussed below—where a practitioner buys another practitioner's practice and makes payments to the selling practitioner over a period of time, while retaining the seller as an employee. (Given that the "bona fide employee" exception is statutory, this interpretation may be open to challenge.)

Referral Services

This safe harbor protects payments to referral services by a practitioner who provides services to referred patients, as long as the payment does not depend on the number of referrals made to that practitioner.[58] Under the safe harbor, any payment or exchange of anything of value between a referral service and a referral service participant is protected if *all* of the following four standards are met:

1. The referral service does not exclude as a participant in the referral service any individual or entity who meets the qualifications for participation.
2. Any payment the participant makes to the referral service is assessed equally against and collected equally from all participants, and is based only on the cost of operating the referral service, and not on the volume or value of the referrals to or business generated by the participants for the referral service for which partial or whole payment may be made under Medicare or a state health program.

3. The referral service imposes no requirements on the manner in which the participant provides services to a referred person, except that the referral service may require that the participant provide services at the same rate it charges other persons not referred by the referral service, or that these services be provided for free or at a reduced charge.

4. The referral service makes the five following disclosures to each person seeking a referral, with each such disclosure maintained by the referral service in a written record certifying such disclosure and signed by either the person seeking the referral or by the individual making the disclosure on behalf of the referral service:

   • the manner in which the referral service selects the participants (e.g., when a pregnant woman asks for an obstetrical referral, the service must disclose how the service selects obstetricians to be qualified to receive referrals);

   • whether the participant has paid a fee to the referral service;

   • the manner in which the referral service selects a particular participant for the person seeking a referral (e.g., on a rotation basis);

   • the nature of the relationship between the referral service and the participants (e.g., the obstetrician is on the active medical staff of a particular hospital); and

   • the nature of any restrictions that would exclude an individual or entity from continuing as a participant (e.g., if a malpractice allegation is raised against the obstetrician or if he or she refuses to treat a certain number of uncompensated cases).

Hospitals frequently provide referral services to their medical staffs without charge. The preamble states that the antikickback statute is implicated even when referrals are paid for within direct forms of remuneration, and that the services physicians furnish hospitals (such as serving on committees) "may constitute a form of remuneration to the hospital for providing the referral service." Therefore, the preamble says, staff physicians and hospitals seeking safe-harbor protection must comply with the standard listed above if they wish to protect a referral service arrangement that does not involve a specific fee.

For hospitals that operate such referral services, the most difficult requirement to meet will be the fourth one. Note the signature requirement to document the required disclosures; the OIG has said that maintaining merely "a blank copy of the disclosure form or instructions to staff on how to make the disclosure" is inadequate. Moreover, the method of disclosure must be deemed "effective disclosure," which "requires that the relevant information is communicated in time for the information to be used by the beneficiary before an important decision is made." Therefore, sending letters containing the disclosure requirements after the fact most likely will be deemed ineffective.

Warranties

Warranties that provide more than the replacement of a defective product can be illegal remuneration under the anti-kickback statute if they are kickbacks for purchasing certain equipment from a manufacturer or supplier. This safe harbor[59] covers warranties that meet the definition of that term in the Magnuson-Moss Warranty-Federal Trade Commission Improvement Act,[60] as well as agreements by a manufacturer or supplier to replace another manufacturer's or supplier's defective item (which is covered by an agreement made in accordance with the same statute), on terms equal to the agreement if replaced.

Standards for Buyers: Any payment or exchange of anything of value under a warranty provided by a manufacturer or supplier of an item to the buyer of the item receives safe-harbor protection as long as the *buyer:*

1. fully and accurately reports any price reduction of the item (including a free item), which was obtained as part of the warranty, in the applicable cost-reporting mechanism or claim for payment filed with HHS or a state agency; and
2. provides, upon request by the Secretary or state agency, the information that manufacturers or suppliers must report, as set forth below.

Standards for Manufacturers and Suppliers: To qualify for the safe-harbor protection, the *manufacturer* or *supplier* must:

1. fully and accurately report the price reduction of the item (including a free item), which was obtained as part of the warranty, on the invoice or statement submitted to the buyer, and inform the buyer of its obligations as indicated above; or
2. where the amount of the price reduction is not known at the time of sale, the manufacturer or supplier must:
   • fully and accurately report the existence of a warranty on the invoice or statement;
   • inform the buyer of its obligations (as described above); and
   • when the price reduction becomes known, provide the buyer with documentation of the calculation of the price reduction resulting from the warranty.
3. the manufacturer or supplier must not pay any remuneration to any entity or individual (other than a beneficiary) for any medical, surgical, or hospital expense incurred by a beneficiary other than for the cost of the item itself.

This regulation, the OIG says, was "based on the Federal Trade Commission interpretation of 15 U.S.C. § 2301(6), which does not require the manufacturer to make full payment to compensate for all costs associated with its defective product." The preamble states the OIG's belief that "warranties generally benefit consumers as well as the Medicare and Medicaid program, even though they may constitute a technical violation of the statute." For that reason, the OIG sees no reason not to cover suppliers who expand the protection afforded by the manufacturer's warranty as long as they comply with this provision. Indeed, "such expanded warranties should be encouraged."

Discounts

This safe harbor allows a seller of goods or services to offer a price discount to a potential purchaser if the transaction is conducted at arm's length, while leaving "bundled" purchases (arrangements that give price reductions to buyers on other goods or services if they purchase one such item) within the ambit of the antikickback statute.[61] "Discount," a key definition in this safe harbor,

- is defined as "a reduction in the amount a seller charges a buyer (who buys either directly or through a wholesaler or a group purchasing organization) for a good or service based on an arm's-length transaction."
- The term "discount" may include a rebate check, credit, or coupon directly redeemable from the seller only to the extent that such reductions in price are attributable to the original good or service that was purchased or furnished.
- The term "discount" does *not* include any cash payment, nor does it include furnishing one good or service without charge or at a reduced charge in exchange for any agreement to buy a different good or service.

Standards for Buyers: A hospital that receives a discount for a good or service it buys must comply with the following four standards to obtain safe-harbor protection:

1. The discount must be earned based on purchases of that same good or service bought within a single fiscal year.
2. The hospital must claim the benefit of the discount in the fiscal year in which the discount is earned or the following year.
3. The hospital must fully and accurately report the discount in the applicable cost report.
4. The hospital must provide, upon request by the Secretary or a state agency, information that sellers are obligated to provide under the regulation.

Standards for Sellers: The person or entity that sells discounted goods or services to a hospital must comply with *either* of the following two standards:

1. the seller must fully and accurately report such discount on the invoice or statement submitted to the buyer, and inform the buyer of its obligations to report such discount; or
2. where the value of the discount is not known at the time of sale, the seller must fully and accurately report the existence of a discount program on the invoice or statement submitted to the buyer, inform the buyer of its obligations to report discounts, and, when the value of the discount becomes known, provide the buyer with documentation

of the calculation of the discount identifying the specific goods or services purchased to which the discount will be applied.

These rules apply to hospital purchases only. The regulation sets forth different requirements if the purchaser is a person or entity other than one—such as a hospital—that reports its costs on a cost report required by HHS or a state agency.

To qualify for the discount safe harbor, transactions must be made on an "arm's-length basis." The preamble notes the OIG's disapproval of "collusive arrangements" involving entities that serve both as a supplier and a joint venture partner with referring physicians, which share profits with the physicians by providing discounts to the joint venture. Similarly, HHS refused to extend the definition of "discount" to include "bundled goods" arrangements (such as a free surgical pack with the purchase of an intraocular lens, or credits toward free computers or other items that might be useful in a physician's practice), on the rationale that there is high potential for abuse in the practice of a seller's giving away, or reducing the price of, one good in connection with the purchase of a different good. The preamble states that the OIG will decide whether to prosecute purchasing practices involving the free provision of another type of item on a case-by-case basis. In such cases, the factors to be considered are:

- the amount of the benefit that was reported and passed along to the programs,
- whether the good is separately reimbursable, and
- the intent behind the arrangement.

The regulations explicitly exempt from the definition of a "discount" the following additional items:

- a reduction in price applicable to one payer but not to Medicare or a state health care program,
- a reduction in price offered to a beneficiary (such as a routine reduction or waiver of any coinsurance or deductible amount owed by a program beneficiary),
- warranties,

- services provided in accordance with a personal or management services contract, and
- other remuneration in cash or in kind not explicitly described in this section of the Safe Harbor Rules.

Discounts for prompt payment should not implicate the statute; however, HHS "will continue to scrutinize closely 'prompt pay' discounts to make sure that they are not payments made for an illegal purpose. . . ." The preamble indicates that the requirement that involves reporting to the program under this safe harbor is satisfied by indicating on the invoice statement, claim, or request for payment that the actual purchase price is "net discount," rather than including all the information in the calculation of the discount.

Employees

This safe harbor allows an employer to pay an employee, who has a bona fide employment relationship with the employer, for providing covered items or services.[62] HHS has adopted the IRS's definition of "employee" for purposes of this safe harbor.[63]

The preamble states that as long as a bona fide employer/employee relationship exists, this safe harbor protects compensation for part-time employment. However, the preamble also makes it clear that this safe harbor does not extend to independent contractors. The OIG recognizes that some state laws may not make it possible for health care providers to enter into arrangements that fall under the IRS definition of "employee," and suggests that these providers seek protection under the provision for personal services and management contracts.

Group Purchasing Organizations

This safe harbor applies to group purchasing organizations (GPOs), which offer providers the opportunity to purchase supplies at reduced prices because of the larger quantities they purchase.[64] It allows any payment by a vendor of goods or services to a GPO, as part of an agreement to furnish such goods or services to an individual or entity, to receive safe harbor protection if:

1. the GPO has a written agreement with each individual or entity for which items or services are furnished; and
   - that agreement states that participating vendors from which the individual or entity will purchase goods or services will pay a fee to the GPO of 3 percent or less of the purchase price of the goods or services provided by that vendor; or
   - if the fee paid to the GPO is not fixed at 3 percent or less of the purchase price of the goods or services, the agreement specifies the amount (or if not known, the maximum amount) the GPO will be paid by each vendor. The fee may be a fixed sum or a fixed percentage of the value of purchases made from the vendor by the members of the group under the contract between the vendor and the GPO; and
2. where the entity that receives the good or service from the vendor is a health care provider of services, the GPO must disclose in writing to the entity at least annually, and to the HHS Secretary upon request, the amount received from each vendor with respect to purchases made by or on behalf of the entity.

The key term, "group purchasing organization," is defined as follows:

> An entity authorized to act as a purchasing agent for a group of individuals or entities who are furnishing services for which payment may be made under Medicare or a State health care program, and who are neither wholly owned by the GPO nor subsidiaries of a parent corporation that wholly owns the GPO (either directly or through another wholly owned entity).

Note that this safe harbor requires that written contracts specify the amount the vendor pays the GPO and that the GPO must disclose to a health care provider the fees it receives from only those vendors that provide goods or services to that provider.

The preamble stresses that this safe harbor applies only to payments made by a vendor of services or goods to a person authorized to act as a GPO; therefore a vendor's discount payments made to a health care provider must qualify under the discount exception to receive protection. HHS also states that it believes Congress did not intend to apply this statutory exception when it is the vendor—not the health care provider—who is furnishing services and directly billing the Medicare or Medicaid program.

Because of the special relationship wholly owned subsidiaries have with their parent corporation, HHS is considering a separate safe harbor for payments between such entities. The preamble notes, however, that it is inappropriate for a chain of facilities (such as nursing homes) to qualify as a GPO and request "GPO fees" for referral of services from chain members.

Waiver of Beneficiary Coinsurance and Deductible Amounts

Under this safe harbor,[65] hospitals may waive copayments or deductibles for inpatient hospital care for which Medicare pays under the PPS, as long as the following three standards are met:

1. The hospital must offer the benefit without regard to the Medicare beneficiaries' reasons for admission, lengths of stay, or their diagnoses.
2. The hospital must not later claim the amount reduced or waived as a bad debt for payment purposes under Medicare, or otherwise shift the burden of the reduction or waiver onto Medicare, a state health program, other payers, or individuals.
3. The hospital must not make the waiver a part of a price reduction agreement between the hospital and a third-party payer.

This safe harbor was amended to except certain agreements entered into between hospitals and a limited group of Medigap insurers (called Medicare SELECT),[66] and has a fairly narrow scope. It does not permit a waiver of coinsurance or deductibles for outpatient services or for hospital units not covered under PPS and does not include physician services. The preamble notes that routine waivers by charge-based providers may affect the program adversely: "When charge-based health care providers routinely fail to collect all or part of beneficiary co-payments authorized by law, and then submit actual charges to Medicare as if copayments amounts were collected, these charges increase customary and prevailing rates which, in turn, inflate program costs." (What impact the fee schedule for physician services will have on this reasoning is not clear.) The preamble reminds parties that the OIG believes that "individuals and entities who fail to reduce actual charges submitted to Medicare are misrepresenting their charges, and may be subject to civil and criminal liability for submitting false claims."

The OIG recognizes that there are situations not covered by this safe harbor provision involving local governmental health care providers (including county hospital outpatient departments), which routinely reduce the beneficiary copayment at the time of service for the extremely indigent population they serve, rather than billing the patients later for the entire copayment. The OIG says that this does not implicate the statute "so long as the partial forgiveness of the copayment obligation was strictly a pragmatic financial decision and not an inducement to patients to purchase medical services."

The preamble stresses that this safe harbor protects the waiver only when the Medicare beneficiaries themselves would have paid the amounts waived. The regulation expressly excludes price reduction agreements between health care providers and third-party payers.

This safe harbor also provides standards (not detailed here) that provide protection for the waiver of copayments and deductibles owed by individuals who qualify by law for subsidized services under Medicaid, the Public Health Services Act, or the Maternal and Child Health Service Block Grant Program, where the services are provided by federally qualifying health centers under Title V (Maternal and Child Health) or Title XIX (Medicaid) of the Social Security Act; or other health care facilities under any Public Health Services Act grant program or under Title V of the Social Security Act.

This safe harbor specifies that a waiver of deductibles and coinsurance for inpatient hospital services covered under PPS will not be considered an illegal referral payment. The HHS OIG, however, sent a Fraud Alert to Medicare providers, physicians, and suppliers in May 1991 warning that charge-based providers, practitioners, and suppliers cannot routinely waive Medicare copayments and deductibles. To do so, according to the OIG, may be interpreted as unlawfully inducing patients to purchase items or services from them. The Fraud Alert does not state a new policy, but may presage more vigorous enforcement activity in this area. It should be noted that the safe harbor regulations do not protect the waiver of Medicare Part B coinsurance and deductible amounts.

Managed Care Safe Harbors

Two additional safe harbors regarding managed care plans were published in the *Federal Register* November 5, 1992.[67]

Both safe harbors incorporate the following definitions:

Enrollee: An individual who has entered into a contractual relationship with a health plan (or on whose behalf an employer, or other private or governmental entity, has entered into such a relationship), under which the individual is entitled to receive specified health care items and services, or insurance coverage for such items and services, in return for payment of a premium.

Contract health care provider: An individual or entity under contract with a health plan to furnish items or services to enrollees who are covered by the health plan, Medicare, or a state health care program.

Health plan means an entity that either:

- furnishes or arranges under agreement with contract health care providers for the furnishing of items or services to enrollees; or
- furnishes insurance coverage for the provision of such items and services in exchange for a premium.

To qualify as a health plan under the proposed regulations, such entity must either:

- operate in accordance with a contract, agreement, or statutory demonstration authority approved by HCFA or a state health care program, or

- have its premium structure regulated under a state insurance statute or a state enabling statute governing HMOs or preferred provider organizations (PPOs).

(This definition thus appears not to cover employer self-insurance plans. It covers ordinary HMOs and PPOs only if the state has state oversight that includes state regulation of the premiums charged to subscribers.)

Increased Coverage, Reduced Cost-Sharing Amounts, or Reduced Premium Amounts Offered by Health Plans to Enrollees

Under this managed care safe harbor,[68] health plans may offer additional coverage of any item or service to an enrollee, reduce some or all of the enrollee's obligation to pay the health plan or a contract health care provider for cost-sharing amounts (such as coinsurance, deductible, or copayment amounts), or reduce the premium amounts attributable to items or services covered by the health plan, Medicare, or a state health plan as long as the health plan complies with all of the standards in one of the following two categories of health plans:

1. If the health plan is a risk-based HMO, a CMP, prepaid health plan, or other health plan under contract with HCFA or state health care program, it must:
   - Offer the same increased coverage or reduced cost-sharing or premium amounts to all enrollees unless otherwise approved by HCFA or by a state health care plan.
2. If the health plan is an HMO, CMP, health care prepayment plan, prepaid health plan, or other health plan that has executed a contract or agreement with HCFA or with a state health program to receive payment for enrollees on a reasonable cost or similar basis, it must:
   - Offer the same increased coverage or reduced cost-sharing or premium amounts to all enrollees unless otherwise approved by HCFA or by a state health plan; and
   - Not claim the costs of the increased coverage or the reduced cost-sharing or premium amounts as a bad debt for payment purposes under Medicare or a state health

care program or otherwise shift the burden of the increased coverage or reduced cost-sharing or premium amounts onto Medicare, a state health care program, other payers, or individuals.

Price Reductions Offered to Health Plans by Providers

Under this safe harbor,[69] contract health care providers may offer a reduction in price to a health plan in accordance with the terms of a written agreement between the contract health care provider and the health plan for the sole purpose of furnishing to enrollees items or services that are covered by the health plan, Medicare, or a state health care program as long as both the health plan and contract health care provider comply with all of the applicable standards within one of the following three categories of health plans:

1. If the health plan is an HMO, CMP, or prepaid health plan under contract with HCFA or a state agency:
   * The contract health provider must not claim payment in any form from the Department or the state agency for items or services furnished in accordance with the agreement except as approved by HCFA or the state health care program, or otherwise shift the burden of such an agreement onto Medicare, a state health care program, other payers, or individuals.
2. If the health plan has executed a contract or agreement with HCFA or a state health care program to receive payment for enrollees on a reasonable-cost or similar basis, the health plan and contract health provider must comply with all of the following four standards:
   * The term of the agreement between the health plan and the contract health care provider *must be for not less than one year.*
   * The agreement between the health plan and the contract health care provider must specify in advance the covered items and services to be furnished to enrollees and the methodology for computing the plan's payment to the contract health care provider.

- The health plan must fully and accurately report, on the applicable cost report or other claim form filed with the Department or the state health care program, the amount it has paid the contract health care provider under the agreement for the covered services furnished to enrollees.
- The contract health care provider must not claim payment in any form from the Department or the state health care program for items or services furnished in accordance with the agreement (except as approved by HCFA or the state health care program), nor may it otherwise shift the burden of such an agreement onto Medicare, a state health care program, other payers, or individuals.

3. If the health plan does not fit into either categories (1) or (2), both the health plan and contract health care provider must comply with all of the following six standards:
   - The term of the agreement between the health plan and the contract health care provider must be for not less than one year.
   - The agreement between the health plan and the contract health care provider must specify in advance the covered items and services to be furnished to enrollees, which party is to file claims or requests for payment with Medicare or the state health care program for such items and services, and the schedule of fees the contract health provider will charge for furnishing such items and services to enrollees.
   - The fee schedule in the agreement between the health plan and the contract health care provider must remain in effect throughout the term of the agreement unless a fee increase results directly from a payment update authorized by Medicare or the state health care program.
   - The party submitting claims or requests for payment from Medicare or the state health program for items and services furnished in accordance with the agreement must not claim or request payment for amounts in excess of the fee schedule.

- The contract health care provider and the health plan must fully and accurately report on any cost report filed with Medicare or a state health care program the fee schedule amounts charged in accordance with the agreement.
- The party to the agreement, which does not have the responsibility under the agreement for filing claims or requests for payment, must not claim or request payment in any form from the Department or the state health care program for items or services furnished in accordance with the agreement, or otherwise shift the burden of such an agreement onto Medicare, a state health care program, other payers, or individuals.

The practical effect of these safe harbors has been questioned by numerous commentators as the regulations seem to protect only transactions that never were seen as violations of the anti-kickback statute in the first place. Some even fear that the regulations are dangerous, based on the concern that it is virtually impossible for any plan to comply fully with all the requirements for safe harbor protection.

Risk-Sharing Arrangements

Of particular importance in a managed care environment is a new exception to the antikickback statute created in the HIPAA.[70] The exception applies to risk-sharing arrangements and significantly expands current safe harbors for managed care agreements. Specifically, the language of the statute states that the new exception applies to any remuneration between an organization or an individual entity providing services, or a combination thereof, pursuant to a written agreement between the organization and the individual if:

- the organization is a Medicare-certified HMO, or
- the written agreement places the individual or entity at substantial financial risk for the cost or utilization of the items or services that the individual or entity is obligated to provide.

The Secretary of HHS is charged with establishing standards to apply this exception on an expedited basis.

SANCTIONS FOR FRAUD AND ABUSE VIOLATIONS

Criminal, civil, and administrative sanctions are available under the Medicare/Medicaid statute to curb fraudulent activities in the health care industry. Depending on the type of activity involved, other federal statutes may serve as enforcement tools, including the False Claims Act and new provisions under the HIPAA.[71]

Criminal Sanctions

Criminal penalties are available under the Medicare/Medicaid statute for submitting false claims and engaging in other fraudulent billing activities. Until 1996, the criminal provisions[72] prohibited knowingly and willfully making or causing to be made any false statement or misrepresentation of material fact in any claim or application for benefits under Medicare or Medicaid.[73] With the enactment of the HIPAA, criminal penalties for fraudulent billing activities became available for all claims under federal health care programs.[74] Examples of prohibited conduct include:

- billing for services not rendered
- misrepresenting the services actually rendered
- falsely certifying that certain services were medically necessary

The statute also prohibits presenting or causing to be presented a claim for physician services, knowing that the individual who furnished the services was not a licensed physician; knowingly and willfully making or causing to be made, or inducing or causing to be induced, the making of any false statements of material facts with regard to an institution's compliance with conditions of participation for the purposes of certification; and knowingly and with fraudulent intent, retaining Medicare and Medicaid funds that were not properly paid.[75]

In addition to the Medicare/Medicaid statute, there are several criminal statutes of more general applicability that can be used to combat the filing of false Medicare and Medicaid statements. For one, the criminal code's False Claims Act makes it illegal to present a claim upon or against the United States that the claimant knows to be "false, fictitious, or fraudulent."[76] (This statute is distinct from the civil FCA.) This statute has been broadly applied to health care fraud, even in situations where the false claim is submitted to an insurance carrier that contracts with the federal government to process Medicare claims.[77]

The Medicare/Medicaid statute also provides for criminal penalties for violations to its antikickback provisions. The antikickback statute, as it was originally enacted in 1972, provided that violations were misdemeanors subject to maximum fines of $10,000 and not more than one year imprisonment. Concluding that these penalties were insufficient to deter health care fraud and abuse, Congress amended the kickback provision in 1977, upgrading the offense to a felony with a maximum fine of $25,000 and a maximum prison term of five years.[78] Prosecutions under the antikickback statute have provided illustrations of how courts will interpret the scope of the prohibition. In *United States v. Greber,*[79] the Third Circuit upheld a physician's criminal conviction under the statute, finding that if even one purpose of a payment is to induce referrals, a violation of the Medicare statute has occurred. The Ninth Circuit endorsed this interpretation in *United States v. Kats,*[80] refusing to allow a defense based on the claim that a payment was made for other purposes besides inducing referrals.

The HIPAA brought significant amendments to federal health care fraud and abuse law, and in particular expanded the range of criminal sanctions available for health care insurance fraud.[81] The new law contains amendments to the criminal code that create new offenses relating to health care fraud. The statute defines the term "federal health care offense," specifying that the offense includes violations or conspiracies to violate specific provisions of the United States Code, where the violation relates to a "health care benefit program." "Health care benefit program" is defined as:

> Any public or private plan or contract, affecting commerce, under which any medical benefit, item or service is provided to any individual, and includes any individual or entity who is providing a medical benefit, item or service for which payment may be made under the plan or contract.[82]

The statute also establishes the offense of "health care fraud," defined as the knowing and willful execution of a scheme to defraud a health care benefit program or obtain through false representations money or other property owned by a health care benefit program. The sanctions available for this offense are fines or a maximum of ten years' imprisonment or both. If the violation results in serious bodily injury, the maximum jail term is life imprisonment.

The statute also amends existing provisions of the code that relate to other offenses, by establishing a specific criminal sanction when these offenses are connected to the delivery of health care services. For example, the statute stipulates that theft or embezzlement in connection with health care can result in a fine or imprisonment of up to ten years, but may not exceed one year if the value of the property involved is less than $100. False statements relating to health care matters can generate fines or a maximum prison sentence of five years or both. Similar sanctions are available for obstructing criminal investigations of health care offenses.

Civil Monetary Penalties

In addition to the various criminal laws that federal prosecutors can use in the war against false Medicare and Medicaid statements and claims, there are also two main civil statutes that can result in major liabilities to fraudulent health care providers. These two statutes closely mirror the two main criminal statutes, as they exist as civil companions to the Medicare/Medicaid statute and the False Claims Act. With civil damages for fraudulent Medicare and Medicaid claims often climbing into the tens of millions of dollars,[83] the civil penalties are potentially just as threatening, if not more so, than the criminal penalties.

Along with the criminal provisions discussed earlier, the Medicare/Medicaid statute also contains provisions for civil monetary sanctions.[84] The Secretary of HHS is authorized by the Civil Monetary Penalty Law (CMPL) to administratively impose civil money penalties and assessments against a person for making false or certain improper claims as defined under that statute.

The HIPAA incorporates a number of significant changes to the civil monetary penalty scheme of the Medicare/Medicaid statute.[85] Consistent with changes to criminal penalties in the statute, civil monetary sanctions are now available for fraudulent activity with respect to the delivery of health care in any federal health care program, not only for Medicare and Medicare claims. Maximum penalties increased from $2,000 to $10,000 and the additional penalty assessment is increased from twice to three times the amount claimed.

The HIPAA provides a definition for the term "should know," stating that the condition is satisfied when a person acts in deliberate ignorance with respect to the information, or acts in reckless disregard of the truth or falsity of the information.[86] The statute clarifies that no proof of specific intent to defraud is required.

Under the 1996 statute, civil monetary penalties are also authorized for offering remuneration to individuals who are eligible for Medicare or Medicaid benefits if the person making the offer knows or should know that the remuneration will influence the patient to order or receive items or services from a particular provider. The statutory definition of "remuneration" includes the waiver of coinsurance and deductible amounts and the provision of items or services at less than fair market value (but a waiver of coinsurance and deductibles is possible under certain statutory requirements). Finally, the new law authorizes the imposition of civil monetary penalties on Medicare HMOs for failing to carry out their contracts or carrying out their contracts in a manner inconsistent with the efficient administration of the program.

Civil monetary provisions in the Medicare/Medicaid statute define the term "person" broadly as including an entity, organization, or agency.[87] Actions may be pursued against individuals, corporations, or partnerships. Moreover, an employer may be held liable for the acts of its employees, such as a billing clerk, if that clerk acted within the scope of his or her employment.

An individual "presents or causes to be presented" a claim by directly or indirectly submitting the claim. For instance, a person is considered to have caused a claim to be presented by signing the certification on the claim form and then having a clerk or the beneficiary submit the claim. For purposes of the statute, a Medicare carrier or intermediary constitutes an agent of the United States.

Under the statute, a "claim" is a request for payment appearing in any form, including written or via electronic transmission. With regard to cost-based providers in the Medicare Part A context, the OIG may base a claim for civil monetary penalties on one of the following: a cost report entry, books of account, or other documents supporting the claim.[88]

With regard to charge-based providers in the Medicare Part B context, the individual items, devices, medical supplies, or services that appear on a claim form may constitute separate itemized claims for payments.[89]

Penalties also can be assessed if the claim is for an item or service furnished during a period in which the person was excluded from the program. It should be noted that the Omnibus Budget Reconciliation Act of 1987 (OBRA '87) changed the statutory language regarding intent from "knows or has reason to know" to "knows or should know." The purpose of this amendment was to stress that those who bill Medicare and Medicaid "have an affirmative duty to ensure that the claims for payment which they submit, or are submitted on their behalf by billing clerks or other employees, are true and accurate representations of the items or services actually provided."[90]

The OIG is concerned that in some cases, an individual or company may submit claims for services that it never furnished to a patient. One scenario may involve a DME company that submits a claim to Medicaid for a wheelchair that it never provided to a patient. In another example, a Medicare beneficiary might conclude her respiratory therapy treatment and request that the supplier pick up the oxygen equipment. In the interim, the DME supplier may be billing Medicare for the rental charge of the oxygen equipment although it is aware that the beneficiary is no longer using the equipment.

Under the statute, the claim must have been "false or fraudulent." Like the civil FCA requirements, the OIG must show only that the claims at issue are false. Several different types of claims may be considered false, such as claims submitted for medically unnecessary services or services not provided as claimed. An example of the latter claim would be a physician who submitted Part B claims for hospital visits that he or she never made. The HIPAA makes clear that upcoding can be sanctioned by civil monetary penalties if an individual engages in this activity with deliberate ignorance or reckless disregard of the truth.[91] Specifically, civil monetary penalties for incorrect codes or medically unnecessary services are available where there is a pattern or practice of presenting or causing to be presented a claim for an item or service that is based on a code that an individual "knows or should know" will result in a greater payment than the code that is applicable to the claim.

In determining the amount or scope of any penalty, assessment, or exclusion, the Secretary is required to take into account the nature of the claims and the circumstances under which they were presented, the degree of culpability, any history of prior offenses, the financial condition of the person presenting the claim, and any other matters as justice may require.[92] Judicial review of the Secretary's final determination is available; in such proceedings, the findings of the Secretary with respect to questions of fact, if supported by substantial evidence on the record considered as a whole, are conclusive.[93]

The Secretary has six years after the date the claim was presented to initiate an action.[94] If the Secretary has reason to believe that any person has engaged, is engaging, or is about to engage in any activity that makes the person subject to a civil monetary penalty under the statute, the Secretary may bring an action in the appropriate U.S. District Court to enjoin such activity.[95]

If a proceeding is being brought against a person who, based on the same transaction, has been convicted (whether upon a verdict after trial or upon a plea of guilty or nolo contendere) of a federal crime charging fraud or false statements, the person is estopped in the civil proceeding from denying the essential elements of the criminal offense.[96] Moreover, because the administrative proceeding under Section 1320a-7a has been held to be civil, and not quasi-criminal in nature, HHS is not required to establish elements of liability beyond a reasonable doubt.[97] Similarly, because the proceedings are civil and not criminal, they have been held to be constitutionally adequate even though the penalty is based on the amount claimed and not on the actual loss sustained by the government.[98]

In basing the penalty on the amount claimed and not on the actual loss, and then adding a fine per false claim, the monetary penalties can be substantial.[99] This was true under the previous civil monetary provisions, and increases in the civil monetary penalties contained in the HIPAA have significantly heightened the risk of potential financial liability under this provision.[100] Because the purpose of the law is to make the government whole for monies paid on fraudulent submissions and the cost of investigating such fraudulent submissions, the amount of actual award that far exceeds these costs has been challenged on constitutional grounds.[101] In *Mayers*,[102] for example, a penalty as high as 70 times greater than the amount actually collected from Medicare for the false claims was held to be constitutional. Another civil statute that can result in major liabilities to health care providers who submit false Medicare or Medicaid claims is the civil FCA.[103] Civil FCA claims against health care providers have risen dramatically in recent years and have resulted in some staggering monetary penalties.[104] One example of this is a settlement in which National Medical Enterprises, Inc., and two of its subsidiaries agreed to pay a total of $379 million in criminal fines and civil damages and penalties to settle a variety of criminal and civil charges involving fraudulent Medicare and Medicaid claims by psychiatric hospitals. $325 million of the settlement was for civil damages and penalties.

The U.S. Supreme Court has held that the government's collection of civil penalties following a Medicare fraud conviction under the civil FCA could violate the Double Jeopardy Clause "to the extent that the second sanction may not fairly be characterized as remedial, but only as a deterrent or retribution. . . ."[105] In *Halper*,[106] the government was seeking to recover a civil penalty of more than $130,000, based on the same 65 false claims that formed the basis for the defendant's criminal conviction. The court possibly did not recognize the frequency with which this situation could occur in the context of the civil monetary penalties provisions of the Medicare Act.

Since *Halper*, however, several courts have ruled that the Double Jeopardy Clause is not implicated in exclusion cases because the purpose of the penalties is remedial, not punitive. In *United States v. Pani*,[107] for example, the court found that the application of civil FCA penalties to three Medicare claims that formed the basis for the physician's criminal conviction for making false claims and conversion did not constitute double jeopardy, because there was a rational relation to the goal of compensating the government for its loss rather than punishing the offender.[108]

The civil FCA states that any person who knowingly presents, or causes to be presented, to the U.S. government, a false or fraudulent claim for payment or approval; knowingly makes, uses, or causes to be made or used, a false record or statement to get a false or fraudulent claim paid or approved by the government; or conspires to defraud the government by getting a false or fraudulent claim allowed or paid violates the Act. Those who violate the Act are liable to the government for a civil penalty of not less than $5,000 and not more than $10,000, plus treble damages sustained by the government, for each false claim filed.[109] No proof of actual damages—such as payment or approval of the claim—is needed to prove a violation of the civil FCA.[110]

The statute defines "knowing" and "knowingly" as meaning the person (1) has actual knowledge of the information, (2) acts in deliberate ignorance of the truth or falsity of the information, or (3) acts in reckless disregard of the truth or falsity of the information.[111] The statute goes on to expressly state that "no proof of specific intent to defraud" is required.[112] Thus, the government is not required to prove actual intent to submit false claims to establish liability under the civil FCA.[113] Rather, the government can establish liability by simply proving deliberate ignorance or reckless disregard for the truth of the claims.[114] However, liability cannot be established based on innocent mistakes or negligence.[115]

The civil FCA's definition of "knowingly" was intended to establish liability of, for example, corporate officers who consciously avoid knowledge of false claims being filed by their subordinates. Moreover, the definition also applies to corporate employees who follow the orders of superiors, or even ignore the activities of coworkers. Thus, both corporate officers and lower-level employees may be liable under the civil FCA for improper claims for which they are aware or should have been aware.[116]

In addition to authorizing the Attorney General to investigate and bring civil actions under the civil FCA, the statute allows a private person (often referred to as a *"qui tam* relator"[117]) to bring a civil action in the name of the United States or the Attorney General against a person or entity for filing a false or fraudulent claim.[118] The purpose of the *qui tam* provisions is to give an incentive for whistleblowers to come forward to help the government discover and prosecute fraudulent claims by awarding them a percentage of the recovery.[119] The provisions are remedial rather than punitive in nature and thus a *qui tam* action brought under the civil FCA survives the death of the plaintiff.[120] Moreover, it has been held that the *qui tam* provisions in no way act to penalize the civil FCA defendant[121] or private persons[122] (referred to as *qui tam* actions).

An action may not be brought more than 6 years after the date on which the violation was committed or more than 3 years after the date when facts material to the right of action are known or reasonably should have been known by the government official charged with responsibility to act in the circumstances (but in no event more than 10 years after the date on which the violation was committed), whichever occurs last.[123]

Since the 1986 False Claims Act Amendments—which served to both enhance individual involvement in initiating false claims actions as well as increase the amount *qui tam* plaintiffs may recover—the number of *qui tam* lawsuits has rapidly increased. As liability may amount to treble damages in addition to $5,000 to $10,000 per false claim, the potential recovery for a *qui tam* plaintiff can be substantial. For instance, a recent settlement of an action brought by the government under the civil FCA against Blue Cross/Blue Shield of Michigan netted the *qui tam* informant $5.5 million.

The antikickback provisions in the Medicare/Medicaid statute do not specifically impose civil monetary penalties for violations of the referral ban, and federal law in general does not authorize the government or private parties to sue for damages for such violations. The government has attempted to circumvent the absence of civil monetary liability for kickback violations by relying on civil sanctions available under a generic federal antikickback law that applies to all government contractors.[124] This statute prohibits offering or accepting compensation to improperly obtain favorable treatment with respect to a government contract, and allows the government to recover civil penalties of twice the amount of each kickback. In *United States v. Kensington Hospital*,[125] however, the court dismissed charges under this statute, ruling that a state Medicaid plan does not constitute a prime/subcontractor agreement within the scope of the statute.

The government has also attempted to invoke the civil FCA to extract a civil remedy from violations of the antikickback statute, arguing that claims for referred services within a relationship that violates the antikickback provision are in fact false or fraudulent. In several *qui tam* suits initiated under the civil FCA, courts have recognized that the Act may be used to recover damages for illegal referrals under the antikickback statute. A federal trial court in Ohio, for example, did not require evidence that the kickback resulted in claims that were false either with respect to the necessity or quality of the services.[126] More recently, a federal trial court in Tennessee allowed a *qui tam* claim to proceed, ruling that illegal referrals under the antikickback statute also constitute violations of the civil FCA.[127] The *qui tam* plaintiff in this case conceded that the illegal referrals were not false in the sense that the health care provider had billed for services that were not provided or unnecessary. He argued, however, that participation in any federal program implies a certification by the participant that it will abide by all the rules governing such a program. The provider's claims in this case were therefore fraudulent, the plaintiff reasoned, because in submitting the claims, the provider acknowledged that it had complied with all the statutory rules governing reimbursement under the Medicare Act, including the federal antikickback and self-referral provisions. The trial court initially disagreed and dismissed the suit, but subsequently reconsidered its decision.

The court ruled that the suit should proceed to trial. The court noted that recent cases support the view that a violation of the Medicare antikickback statute also constitutes a violation of the civil FCA. These cases conclude that the civil FCA covers not only claims that are themselves false, but also claims that derive from fraudulent conduct. The court observed that in this case, the government had not suffered any pecuniary loss because of the provider's alleged illegal activities. Relying on the legislative history of the statute, however, the court ruled that the civil FCA is intended to govern not only fraudulent acts that create a loss to the government, but also fraudulent acts that cause the government to pay sums of money to claimants it did not intend to benefit. The claim in this case alleges that the government would not have paid the claims submitted by the provider if it had been aware of the antikickback and self-referral violations, and suggests that the providers concealed their illegal activities from the government to defraud it into paying claims it would not have otherwise paid. This is sufficient to state a claim under the civil FCA, the court stated, cautioning that to succeed, the evidence will have to establish that the provider engaged in the fraudulent conduct to induce payment from the government. If the provider's fraudulent conduct was not carried out to induce such payment, then the conduct would not taint their Medicare claims and render them false within the meaning of the civil FCA, the court concluded.

Exclusion from the Program

Exclusion of a provider from the Medicare and Medicaid programs can be either mandatory or permissive, depending on the statutory offense involved.

Mandatory Exclusion

Pursuant to the Medicare and Medicaid Patient and Program Protection Act of 1987,[128] any individual or entity convicted of a criminal offense relating to the delivery of services under Medicare or a state health care program, or convicted under federal or state law of a criminal offense related to neglect or abuse of patients in connection with the delivery of a health care item or service, had to be excluded from Medicare, Medicaid, and state health care programs that receive federal funds under the Maternal and Child Health Block Grant or the Social Services Block Grant. Under the HIPAA, exclusion is now mandatory for any felony conviction relating to health care fraud, theft, embezzlement, or other financial misconduct in connection with the delivery of a health care item or service involving any governmental health care program.[129]

A number of courts have addressed the issue of whether exclusion from the Medicare program constitutes a denial of due process. Generally, the courts have found that the exclusion procedures are constitutionally sufficient.[130] This provision applies not only to Medicare and Medicaid patients, but to all patients.

The final regulations, like the Act, state that a mandatory exclusion will be imposed for a minimum period of five years. The regulations also contain aggravating and mitigating circumstances, however, that can be used to establish the appropriate exclusion period.[131]

Aggravating factors under the regulations are as follows:

- The acts produced a loss to Medicare and the state health care programs of $1,500 or more.
- The acts were committed over a period of one year or more.
- The acts had a significant adverse physical, mental, or financial impact on one or more program beneficiaries or others.
- The sentence for the crime included imprisonment.
- The convicted individual or entity has a prior criminal, civil, or administrative sanction record.
- The convicted individual or entity has been overpaid a total of $1,500 or more by Medicare or state health care programs as a result of improper billing.

Mitigating factors under the regulations are as follows:

- The person or entity was convicted of three or fewer misdemeanor offenses, and the amount of loss to Medicare and the state health care programs is less than $1,500.
- The court had determined that the individual had a mental, emotional, or physical condition before or during the commission of the offense.
- The individual's or entity's cooperation with federal or state officials resulted in convictions or exclusions of others or the imposition of civil monetary penalties.

Mitigating factors are considered only if the aggravating factors justify an exclusion of more than five years. The mitigating factors do not reduce the sentence below the five-year minimum.

Permissive Exclusion

In addition, HHS may, in its discretion, exclude from participation in Medicare, and direct states to exclude from participation in state health care programs, any individual or entity that commits specified offenses. These offenses include:

- *Fraud.* A criminal offense in relation to fraud, theft, embezzlement, breach of fiduciary responsibility, or other financial misconduct in connection with the delivery of any health care item or service, or with respect to an act or omission in a program operated or financed by a federal, state, or local government agency.[132]
- *Obstruction of an Investigation.* Interference with, or obstruction of, any investigation into a criminal offense related to Medicare or Medicaid services, patient neglect or abuse, or health care fraud.[133]
- *Suspension or Exclusion under a Federal or State Health Care Program.* Suspension or exclusion from participation, or otherwise sanctioned, under a federal or state health care program for reasons bearing on the individual's or entity's professional competence, professional performance, or financial integrity.[134]
- *Excessive Claims or Furnishing of Unnecessary or Substandard Items and Services.* Submission of bills for payments under

Medicare or a state health care program containing charges or costs for items or services furnished that are substantially in excess of the individual's or entity's usual charges or costs for such items or services, or furnishing to patients items or services substantially in excess of the patient's needs, or of a quality that fails to meet professionally recognized standards of health care.[135]

- *False or Improper Claims.* Filing a false or improper claim with Medicare or a state health program. The imposition of a civil money penalty is not a prerequisite for exclusion.[136]
- *Fraud, Kickbacks, and Other Prohibited Activities.* Violating the Medicare/Medicaid antikickback statute.[137]
- *Entities Owned or Controlled by a Sanctioned Person.* An entity may be excluded if it is owned or controlled by an individual who has been convicted of a Medicare- or Medicaid-related criminal offense, has had civil money penalties imposed, or has been excluded from a federal or state health care program.[138]
- *Failure To Disclose Information.* Failure to disclose information that must be disclosed under the Medicare or Medicaid Acts or regulations.[139]

Persons or entities excluded from program participation under the mandatory exclusions are subject to a minimum exclusion of five years unless the Secretary waives that mandatory period because the individual or entity is a sole community provider or the sole source of essential specialized services in a community. (The Secretary is not empowered to waive the minimum exclusion period when the exclusion is for patient abuse or neglect.)

Prior to the enactment of the HIPAA, the term of permissive exclusion was discretionary, to be specified by the Secretary. Under the new law, minimum periods of exclusion are established for certain categories of convictions.[140] For example, a minimum exclusion period of three years will be required for convictions of misdemeanor criminal health care offenses or convictions relating to obstruction of an investigation. A minimum of one-year exclusion will be required for activities relating to professional competence or financial integrity.

The Effect of an Exclusion Sanction

For an individual, an exclusion sanction results in the inability of that practitioner, or any other entity, to be able to receive reimbursement for any items or services furnished by that practitioner to program beneficiaries on or after the effective date of the exclusion.[141] In addition, no funds from Medicare, state health care programs, or any Executive Branch procurement or nonprocurement programs can be used to reimburse for any items or services ordered by an excluded physician.[142] For example, the effect of an exclusion is so broad that Medicaid will not reimburse for a prescription drug ordered by a physician for a Medicaid beneficiary. An excluded practitioner is prohibited from billing his or her services through the Medicare provider number of another physician. Such a practice risks the OIG pursuing a civil money penalties action. The OIG publishes and distributes an annual report that lists all excluded individuals and entities.

An exclusion can pose different consequences for a corporate entity. For instance, the OIG can impose an exclusion on an entity that was convicted or accepted a guilty plea, and the exclusion applies only to that entity and any of its subsidiaries. Unlike individual practitioners, corporations can shift assets from one entity into another entity to avoid the effect of the exclusion sanction.

Reinstatement

At or near the end of the exclusion period, excluded individuals and entities must submit a written request for reinstatement to the OIG.[143]

Once the OIG receives the written request, it requires that the requestor provide specific information as well as authorization for the OIG to obtain information from a variety of sources, such as private health insurers, peer review bodies, probation officers, and professional colleagues.[144] The reinstatement determination rests fully in the discretion of the OIG based on a number of factors, such as the requestor's conduct during the exclusion period. The regulations prohibit administrative or judicial review of its reinstatement determinations.[145]

Medicare Suspension of Payments

The regulations give Medicare carriers and intermediaries broad authority to suspend all or part of payments to a provider or supplier.[146]

Generally, the carrier or intermediary is required to send out a written notice of an intention to suspend payments and permit a 15-day response period to the supplier or provider.[147]

If the carrier or intermediary has reliable evidence that the provider or supplier's billing practices involve fraud or misrepresentation, then no notice and response period need be given.[148]

A provider cannot appeal the suspension of payments, but is permitted merely to forward a written statement to the carrier or intermediary. If there is a question of possible fraud or misrepresentation, then the provider may not even be afforded the opportunity to present a statement to be considered.[149]

Because the regulations fail to give the provider or supplier any meaningful appeal rights, the government can utilize this tool as leverage against a provider. If a large percentage of a provider's or supplier's total volume comprises Medicare reimbursement, then its entire business may be placed in jeopardy.

POTENTIAL FRAUD AND ABUSE SITUATIONS UNDER PHYSICIAN SELF-REFERRAL LEGISLATION (Stark I and Stark II)

In addition to the Medicare and Medicaid Fraud and Abuse statute, federal law regulates patient referrals between a physician and an entity in which the physician (or an immediate family member) has a financial interest. The Ethics in Patient Referrals Act, commonly referred to as Stark I, was enacted as part of OBRA '89[150] and became effective January 1, 1992. The legislation was adopted in response to concerns about conflicts of interest that could arise when a physician has a financial relationship with a facility and refers patients to that facility for care, and about the inadequacy of existing antifraud and abuse legislation in eliminating the ethical problems associated with patient referrals.

Stark I prohibited a physician investor or a physician having a financial relationship with an entity from making a referral to that entity for clinical laboratory services that are reimbursed under Medicare.[151] In August 1993, as part of OBRA '93, Congress amended the Stark law prohibition to apply to referrals for a much expanded list of health care services, in an enactment commonly referred to as Stark II. The self-referral legislation as it now stands generally states that if a physician has a relationship with an entity:

- The physician may not make a referral for any designated health care service that is reimbursable by Medicare or Medicaid.
- The entity that provides the services may not present a bill to Medicare or Medicaid for services provided as a result of a prohibited referral.

The legislation provides penalties for illegal referrals, including the denial of payment, civil monetary penalties, and program exclusion penalties.[152] Stark II became effective January 1, 1995. Regulations under Stark I were finalized in August 1995.[153]

Scope of the Prohibition

Several key definitions establish the scope of the referral prohibition in the Stark law. First, the notion of "referral" as it is defined in the statute determines when a physician, in the course of caring for a patient, actually refers the patient to other entities The second definition, "designated health services," enumerates the types of health care services to which the prohibition applies. The third definition, "financial relationship," establishes the type of financial interest that must exist between a referral physician (or an immediate family member of that physician) and the provider of the designated health service for the prohibition to apply. In analyzing physician referral activity under the Stark law, therefore, it is necessary to ask:

- Is the referral of a Medicare or Medicaid patient for the provision of a designated health service?

- Is there a financial relationship between the referring physician and the entity that will provide the health care service?

If the answer to both of these questions is affirmative, then the referral is prohibited, unless one of the exceptions discussed below applies.

"Referral"

The notion of referral under the Stark law is broad. It includes the request by a physician for any Part B item or service, including for a consultation with another physician, and any test or procedure ordered by or to be performed by or under the supervision of the other physician.[154]

Accordingly, a physician's request for a consultation with another physician is considered a referral, and any tests or services ordered by the consulting physician will be considered to have been ordered by the referring physician. In addition, the request or establishment of a plan of care by a physician that includes the provision of any of the designated health services constitutes a referral under the law. Therefore, a physician makes a referral whenever an item or service is ordered, even if the service or item will be provided within that same physician's practice. The definition of "referral" does not apply, however, to requests by (1) a pathologist for clinical laboratory tests and pathological examination services, (2) a radiologist for diagnostic radiology services, or (3) a radiation oncologist for radiation therapy if the services are furnished by or under the supervision of such pathologist, radiologist, or radiation oncologist pursuant to a consultation requested by another physician.[155]

"Designated Health Service"

The Stark law bans referral of Medicare or Medicaid patients for any of the following items or services:

- clinical laboratory services
- physical therapy services
- occupational therapy services

- radiology services including magnetic resonance imaging, computerized axial tomography scans, and ultrasound services[156]
- radiation therapy services
- durable medical equipment
- parenteral and enteral nutrients, equipment, and supplies
- prosthetics, orthotics, and prosthetic devices
- home health services
- outpatient prescription drugs
- inpatient and outpatient hospital services[157]

"Financial Relationship"

"Financial relationship" refers to either an "ownership or investment" interest in the entity or a "compensation arrangement" between the physician (or an immediate family member of the physician) and the entity.[158]

An ownership or investment interest may exist through equity, debt, or other means. A financial relationship exists if the physician has an interest in an entity that holds an ownership or investment interest in the entity providing the designated health service. The ownership or investment interest therefore includes related entities. For example, a physician owning an interest in a hospital that in turn owns an investment interest in a home health agency would fall within the scope of the Stark II prohibition.

"Compensation arrangement" is broadly defined to include any remuneration, direct or indirect, overt or covert, in cash or in kind between a physician (or an immediate family member of the physician) and an entity providing designated services.[159] The Stark I statute did not indicate clearly whether "compensation arrangement" included any arrangement regardless of which way the money flowed. In Stark II, however, certain arrangements in which physicians pay an entity for services are specifically included in exceptions to the self-referral prohibition. The statute implicitly indicates that the definition includes arrangements in which the physician pays the entity some form of remuneration. The law also illustrates other forms of remuneration, including the forgiveness of amounts owed for inaccurate tests or the correction of minor billing errors.[160]

Other Definitions

A number of terms used in the legislation are defined in a final rule issued by HCFA under Stark I.[161] "Immediate family member," for instance, includes the husband or wife, natural or adoptive parent, child, sibling, stepparent, stepchild, stepbrother or stepsister, father-in-law, mother-in-law, son-in-law, daughter-in-law, grandparent, grandchild, and spouse of a grandparent or grandchild. The final rule also defines "entity" as a sole proprietorship, trust, corporation, partnership, foundation, not-for-profit corporation, or unincorporated association. "Hospital" under the final rule includes any separate, legally organized, operating entity, plus any subsidiary, related, or other entity that performs services for hospital patients and for which the hospital bills. A hospital does not include entities that perform services for hospital patients "under arrangements" with the hospital. "Direct supervision" is defined as supervision by a physician who is present in the office suite and immediately available to provide assistance and direction throughout the time that services are being performed. This definition clarifies that physician practices need not employ the individuals performing the laboratory tests, incorporating retroactive changes made by Stark II to Stark I.

Exceptions to the Prohibition

The statutory exceptions to the general prohibition are numerous and complex. Indeed, Stark is largely a statute of exception; once the general prohibition is understood, the exceptions become critical to compliance.[162] The exceptions can be divided into three categories: (1) those that apply to ownership or investment financial relationships, (2) those that apply to compensation arrangements, and (3) general exceptions that apply to all types of financial relationships.

Exceptions Relating to Both Ownership or Investment and Compensation Arrangements

The following is an enumeration of the exceptions to the ban on self-referral that apply to all types of financial relationships.

Physician Services

The Stark law prohibition on referrals does not apply when services are provided personally (or under the personal supervision of) the referring physician or by another physician in the same group practice[163] as the referring physician.[164]

In-Office Ancillary Services

Because the definition of referral covers situations where a physician orders a test and then performs it within the scope of his or her practice, the in-office ancillary services exception is particularly important in this context. Certain ancillary services provided personally by the referring physician or another physician in the same group practice[165] are exempted from the self-referral prohibition as long as the services satisfy the conditions set out in the statute. First, the service must be provided either personally by the referring physician, personally by a physician who is a member of the same group practice as the referring physician, or personally by individuals who are directly supervised by the referring physician or another physician member of the group practice. The statute also imposes a location requirement, stipulating that the service must be provided either in a building in which the referring physician (or another physician who is a member of the same group practice) furnishes physician services unrelated to the provision of designated health services; or (if the referring physician is a member of a group practice) in another building that is used by the group practice for the provision of some or all of the group's clinical laboratory services, or for the centralized provision of the group's designated health services (other than clinical laboratory service). Finally, to qualify under the in-office ancillary services exception, the services must be billed either by the physician who performs or supervises them, by a group practice of which such physician is a member under a billing number assigned to the group practice, or by an entity that is wholly owned by such physician or such group practice.[166]

The in-office ancillary services exception does not apply to the provision of DME except for infusion pumps, nor to parenteral and enteral nutrients, equipment, and supplies. With respect to shared laboratories, HCFA provides an illustration of how physicians involved in these relationships might comply with the law under the in-office ancillary services exception in the preamble to the final rule it issued under Stark I.[167] The rule does not contain any specific exception for shared laboratories, however. In one example of a shared laboratory arrangement, several physicians set up a laboratory separate from their practices, share in its operating costs, and bill individually for services provided by the laboratory to their own patients. Because the physicians each have an ownership interest in the laboratory, they would not be able to refer to the laboratory unless they qualify for an exception under Stark I. The preamble indicates that the in-office ancillary service exception could apply in this example if each individual physician meets the location, billing, and supervision requirements contained in this exception. In another example, three independent solo practitioners, with offices in the same building, may bill for services furnished to their own patients who are referred to a shared laboratory located in that building, as long as all the requirements of the in-office ancillary services exception are met. This implies that each referring physician personally must perform or directly supervise the performance of the laboratory tests that he or she has ordered and that each physician must bill for the services provided to his or her own patients. In the case of a laboratory shared between two group practices, however, HCFA indicates that neither of the practices would be permitted to bill for the referrals made to the shared laboratory. HCFA states that individual physicians in either group may bill for a test they refer to the shared laboratory, if the physician personally performs or directly supervises the test.

Definition of "Group Practice"

Satisfying the requirements of these first two general exceptions (physicians' services and in-office ancillary services) depends in large part on whether a group or collection of physicians qualifies as a group practice under the statute. "Group practice" means a group of two or more physicians legally organized as a partnership, professional corporation, foundation, not-for-profit corporation, faculty practice plan, or similar association. Members of a group practice may include partners, full-

and part-time employees, and contract physicians. If a facility is legally organized to include two or more physicians and provides the services of physicians, it may still qualify as a group practice, even if it is not established, operated, and controlled by a physician group or corporation. A practice must satisfy the conditions enunciated in the law itself and the regulations adopted under Stark I.[168] These conditions include the following. A significant requirement in meeting the definition of "group practice" is that each physician who is a member of the group must provide substantially the full range of services that the physician routinely provides (including medical care, consultation, diagnosis, or treatment) through the joint use of shared office space, facilities, equipment, and personnel. In addition, substantially all of the services of the physicians who are members of the group must be provided through the group and billed under a billing number assigned to the group, and the receipts for these services must be treated as receipts for the group. The "substantially all" requirement is delineated in the final rule issued by HCFA under Stark I,[169] with the specification that 75 percent of the total patient care services performed by the group practice members must be furnished through the group, billed in the name of the group, and treated as the receipts of the group. "Patient care services" refers to any tasks performed by a group member that address the medical needs of specific patients, regardless of whether they involve direct patient encounters. The 75 percent of the total patient care services represents a reduction from the 85 percent minimum requirement that had been incorporated in the 1992 proposed regulations, and does not apply to group practices located in health professional shortage areas as defined in the Public Health Service Act.

The final rule also addresses how the percentage of patient care services is to be measured, indicating that the calculation is based on the total patient care time each member spends on these services. An illustration provided in the preamble to the rule describes a group practice comprising 10 physicians who deliver patient services. Eight of the 10 physicians devote 100 percent of their total patient care time to the group practice, while another physician devotes 80 percent and another only

10 percent. HCFA illustrates that together, the 10 physicians devote 890 percent of their total time to the group practice. When this figure is divided by the number of physicians in the group, the result is that 89 percent of their combined services are provided through the group, satisfying the 75 percent "substantially all" requirement set out in the final rule.

Other conditions for meeting the definition of "group practice" include:

- The overhead expenses of and the income from the practice must be distributed in accordance with methods previously determined.
- No physician who is a member of the group may receive, either directly or indirectly, compensation based on the volume or value of referrals by the physician.
- Members of the group must personally conduct no less than 75 percent of the physician-patient encounters of the group practice.[170]

As indicated, physicians may not be compensated based on the value or volume of their referrals with the exception of two special rules relating to the compensation of physicians in the group practice. A physician in a group practice may be paid a share of overall profits of the group, or a productivity bonus based on services personally performed or services incident to personally performed services, as long as the share or bonus is not determined in any manner that is directly related to the volume or value of referrals by such physician. In the case of a faculty practice plan associated with a hospital, institution of higher education, or medical school with an approved medical residency training program in which physician members may provide a variety of different specialty services as well as professional services both within and outside the group, and perform other tasks such as research, the group practice definition applies only with respect to the services provided within the faculty practice plan.[171]

A group practice that meets the statutory definition under the statute and the final rule must submit an annual written statement to its Medicare carrier attesting that during the most recent 12-month period, it met the 75 percent patient care services requirement. Groups may select whether they wish to use the fiscal year, the calendar year, or the 12-month period immediately preceding for reporting purposes. Once a group selects a 12-month period, it must adhere to its choice. The original deadline for filing an attestation was no later than 120 days after Aug. 14, 1995. HCFA subsequently changed the date by which a group of physicians wishing to qualify as a group practice under Stark I regulations must file the statement with the agency indicating that it meets the rule requirements for this purpose. On December 11, 1995, HCFA published an amendment to the rule, delaying the notice provision for 60 days after a group receives attestation instructions from its carrier.[172]

Prepaid Plans

The third general exception covers services provided by various prepaid plans. It provides that the physician self-referral ban does not apply to federally qualified HMOs[173] or similar entities recognized by federal law. Such entities include those with contracts under Section 1876 of the Social Security Act, plans described in Section 1833(a)(1)(A) of the Social Security Act, and plans that receive payments on a prepaid basis under demonstration projects as described in either Section 402(a) of the Social Security Amendments of 1967 or Section 222(a) of the Social Security Amendments of 1972.

Exceptions Relating Only to Ownership or Investment Arrangements

The following is an enumeration of the exceptions to the ban on self-referral that apply only to ownership/investment arrangements.

Ownership in Publicly Traded Securities and Mutual Funds

For purposes of the Stark statute, ownership of investment securities or shares in a required investment company, if certain statutory conditions are met, does not qualify as a financial relationship. Ownership of investment securities (including shares or bonds, debentures, notes, or other debt instruments), which may be purchased on terms generally available to the public, qualifies under this exception if the securities are:

- listed on the New York Stock Exchange, the American Stock Exchange, or any regional exchange in which quotations are published daily, or are foreign securities listed on a recognized, foreign, national, or regional exchange in which quotations are published daily, or are traded under an automated interdealer quotation system operated by the National Association of Securities Dealers, and

- in a corporation that, at the end of its most recent fiscal year or on average during the previous three fiscal years, had stockholder equity exceeding $75 million.

Ownership of shares in a regulated investment company (as defined in Section 851(a) of the Internal Revenue Code) also will qualify under this exception if the company, at the end of its most recent fiscal year or on average during the previous three fiscal years, had total assets exceeding $75 million.[174]

Ownership Interest in Hospitals

The Stark legislation ban on self-referral does not apply to designated health services provided by a hospital if the referring physician is authorized to perform services at the hospital and the physician's ownership or investment interest is in the hospital itself and not simply one of its subdivisions or departments.[175]

Rural Providers

The self-referral ban does not apply to designated health services furnished in a rural area[176] by an entity if substantially all of such services provided by the entity are furnished to individuals who reside in the rural area. A physician therefore can refer patients to an entity with which he or she has a financial relationship if the entity is located in a rural area and primarily serves patients residing in that same area.[177] The wording of this exception reflects legislative intent to prevent providers from attempting to fall within the exception by moving their locations to the boundary of a rural area while continuing to serve patients in a nonrural area.

Hospitals in Puerto Rico

The Stark II prohibition does not apply to designated health services provided by hospitals in Puerto Rico.[178]

Exceptions Relating to Compensation Arrangements

Specific compensation arrangements defined in Stark II will not be considered financial relationships that trigger the self-referral ban as long as the arrangements meet the conditions outlined in the statute. These compensation arrangements can be categorized as follows.

Rental of Office Space and Equipment

Payments made by a lessee to a lessor for the use of office space or equipment are not included in the self-referral ban if:

- the lease is in writing, is signed by the parties and indicates the space/equipment covered by the lease
- the space/equipment rented or leased does not exceed what is reasonable and necessary for the legitimate business purposes of the lease or rental, and is used exclusively by the lessee when being used by the lessee
- the lessee, with respect to office space rentals, may pay for the use of space consisting of common areas if the payments do not exceed the lessee's pro rata share of expenses for such space based on the ratio of space used exclusively by the lessee to the total amount of space (other than the common areas) occupied by all persons using such common areas
- the term of the lease is for at least one year
- the rental charges over the term of the lease are set in advance, are consistent with fair market value, and are not calculated in any way on the basis of the volume or value of referrals or other business between the parties
- the lease would be commercially reasonable even if no referrals were made between the parties
- the lease meets any other requirements that the Secretary of HHS may impose by regulation to protect against program or patient abuse.[179]

Bona Fide Employment Relationships

The self-referral ban does not apply to any amount paid by an employer to a physician (or a member of the physician's immediate family) if the physician (or family member) has a bona fide employment relationship with the employer for the provision of services, as long as:

- the employment is for identifiable services
- the remuneration is consistent with the fair market value of the services and is not determined in any manner that takes into account the volume or value of any referrals made by the referring physician
- the remuneration is provided under an agreement that would be commercially reasonable even if no referrals were made to the employer
- the employment meets any other requirements the Secretary of HHS may impose by regulation as needed to protect against program or patient abuse[180]

In bona fide employment relationships, the law expressly allows remuneration in the form of a productivity bonus as long as the bonus is based on services performed personally by the physician (or by an immediate family member of the physician). Unlike the type of compensation permitted in the definition of "group practice," the productivity bonus under this exception cannot be based on services provided under the referring physician's supervision, and it cannot include sharing in the group's profits.

Personal Service Arrangements

The ban on self-referral does not apply to remuneration from an entity under an arrangement for the provision of physician services (including remuneration for specific physicians' services furnished to a nonprofit blood center) if:

- the arrangement is in writing, signed by the parties, and specifies the services it covers
- the arrangement covers all of the services to be provided by the physician (or an immediate family member of such physician) to the entity

- the aggregate services contracted for do not exceed those that are reasonable and necessary for the legitimate business purposes of the arrangement
- the term of the arrangement is for at least one year
- the compensation to be paid over the term of the arrangement is set in advance, does not exceed fair market value and, except in the case of a PIP described below, is not determined in a manner that takes into account the volume or value of any referrals or other business generated between the parties
- the services to be performed under the arrangement do not involve the counseling or promotion of a business arrangement or other activity that violates any state or federal law
- the arrangement meets any other requirements the Secretary of HHS may impose as needed to protect against program or patient abuse[181]

The statute creates a special rule with respect to PIPs for this exception. "Physician incentive plans" are defined as any compensation arrangement between an entity and a physician or physician group that directly or indirectly may have the effect of reducing or limiting services provided with respect to individuals enrolled with the entity.[182]

Under this rule, if a PIP meets the conditions set out in the statute, then the compensation paid under the terms of a personal services arrangement may be determined in a manner that takes into account, either directly or indirectly, the volume or value of any referrals or other business between the parties. To qualify under this rule, the plan must meet the following requirements:

- No specific payment may be made directly or indirectly under the plan to a physician or a physician group as an inducement to reduce or limit medically necessary services provided to a specific individual enrolled with the entity.
- A plan that places a physician or a physician group at substantial financial risk as determined by the Secretary under Section 1876(i)(8)(A)(ii) must comply with any requirements the Secretary may impose pursuant to such section.

- The entity, upon request by the Secretary, must provide HHS with access to descriptive information regarding the plan in order to permit the Secretary to determine whether it is in compliance with the above requirements.[183]

Remuneration Unrelated to Designated Services

Remuneration provided by a hospital to a physician that does not relate to the provision of designated health services is not a compensation arrangement to which the ban on self-referral applies.[184]

Physician Recruitment

If a hospital provides remuneration to a physician to induce the physician to relocate to the geographic area served by the hospital and to join the hospital's medical staff, the Stark prohibition will not apply as long as:

- the physician is not required to refer patients to the hospital
- the amount of the remuneration is not determined in a manner that takes into account directly or indirectly the volume or value of any referrals by the referring physician
- the arrangement meets any other requirements the Secretary may impose by regulation to protect against program or patient abuse[185]

It is important to note that this exception protects only incentives paid to physicians to relocate their practices to a new service area. It does not cover incentives paid to retain physicians or incentives paid to physicians who do not have existing practices.

Isolated Transactions

An exception to the self-referral ban also applies to one-time transactions, such as the one-time sale of a property or practice, if:

- the amount of the remuneration paid under the transaction is consistent with fair market value, and is not based, either directly or indirectly, on the volume or value of any referrals by the referring physician

- the remuneration is provided under an agreement that would be commercially reasonable even if no referrals were made to the entity
- the arrangement meets any other requirements the Secretary may impose by regulation in order to protect against program or patient abuse[186]

In HCFA's final rule governing physician referral under Stark I,[187] the definition of "isolated transactions" enunciates other conditions that a financial relationship must meet to qualify under this exception. The final regulations prohibit a financial relationship between the parties for six months following the isolated transaction, unless the new financial relationship itself qualifies for a separate exception under the law. The regulations also specify that the transaction must involve a single payment and that installment payments or other long-term payment arrangements will not meet the requirements of this exception.

Certain Group Practice Arrangements with a Hospital

The self-referral ban does not apply to an arrangement between a hospital and a group for designated health services to be provided by the group but billed by the hospital if:

- the arrangement is pursuant to the provision of inpatient services under Section 1861(b)(3)
- the arrangement began before December 19, 1989, and has continued uninterrupted since that date
- the group provides, under the arrangement, substantially all of the designated health services covered by the arrangement that are furnished to hospital patients
- the arrangement is pursuant to a written agreement that specifies the services to be provided and the compensation for the services
- the compensation is provided pursuant to an agreement that would be commercially reasonable even if no referrals were made to the entity

- the arrangement between the parties meets any other requirements the Secretary may impose by regulation to protect against program or patient abuse[188]

Payments by a Physician for Items and Services

The self-referral ban does not apply to payments made by a physician to a laboratory for the provision of clinical laboratory services, or to an entity as compensation for other items or services, if the prices of the items or services are consistent with fair market value.[189] By not applying the fair market value standard to clinical laboratory services, the statute implicitly recognizes the heavy discounting practices prevalent in this industry.

De Minimis Remuneration

One final exception to the Stark prohibition can be found in the definition of the term "remuneration."[190]

The statute provides that the forgiveness of amounts owed for inaccurate tests or procedures or the correction of minor billing errors are not considered "remuneration" under the law. In the same manner, the provision of items used solely to collect, transport, process, or store specimens of the entity performing the diagnostic tests or to order or communicate the results of these tests or procedures are not "remuneration."

Reporting Requirements

The Stark law imposes reporting requirements for covered items or services that are paid for under the Medicare/Medicaid program. These entities must provide the Secretary of HHS with information concerning their ownership arrangements, including: (1) the covered items and services they provide, and (2) the names and individual physician identification numbers of all physicians who have an ownership or investment interest in the entity or whose immediate relatives have such an interest in the entity. According to regulations adopted under Stark I and finalized by HCFA, entities that are subject to the reporting requirements must submit the required information on a HCFA-prescribed form within the time period specified by the servicing carrier or intermediary. All entities will be given at least 30 days from the date of the carrier's or intermediary's request to provide the initial information. All entities must retain documentation sufficient to verify the information provided on the forms, and make the information available to HCFA or the OIG upon request. Failure to submit the information in accordance with the regulations can result in fines of up to $10,000 for each day of the period following the deadline for submission of the information until the information is finally submitted.[191]

Sanctions

Stark II enumerates the sanctions that may be imposed for referrals made or claims submitted in violation of the self-referral ban. They include:

- denial of payment
- requirement for refunds for certain claims
- civil monetary penalties
- exclusion from the program[192]

Distinction Between Antikickback and Self-Referral Legislation

Although the Medicare and Medicaid Antikickback statute and the self-referral legislation both attempt to eliminate what are perceived as unacceptable conflicts of interest that exist when a provider has a financial relationship with an entity to which the provider refers patients, it is important to analyze the statutes separately. Compliance with both statutes is necessary to operate lawfully within the Medicare and Medicaid programs. The fact that a relationship falls within an antikickback safe harbor does not determine whether a Stark violation has occurred. Similarly, falling within a Stark exception does not protect against possible antikickback violations. The statutes can be distinguished in several ways.

The Stark law is not a criminal statute, while the antikickback statute is. Under the antikickback statute, evidence of a corrupt intent is necessary to prove a violation under the law; intent is irrelevant in a Stark law analysis. The antikickback law imposes criminal sanctions for specified offenses, including fines and prison sentences, the amount and duration of which vary depending on whether the violation is classified as a misdemeanor or a felony.

The Stark law has been described as an "exceptions bill," meaning that it establishes a broad prohibition on certain categories of referrals, but permits numerous exceptions. If a particular service or financial relationship is covered by one of the exceptions discussed above, the referral is not prohibited. If no exception applies, however, the referral is illegal and Medicare/Medicaid will not reimburse the cost of the service. The antikickback statute does not prohibit certain referrals per se. Rather it forbids any knowing and willful conduct involving the solicitation, receipt, offer, or payment of any kind of remuneration in return for referring an individual or for recommending or arranging the purchase, lease, or ordering of an item or service that may be paid for wholly or partly through the Medicare/Medicaid program. The safe harbors under the antikickback statute are not mandatory, in that an arrangement must fit into a safe harbor to comply with the law. Rather, the safe harbors exist to provide absolute immunity to specific arrangements that are free from abuse. If a safe harbor does not apply, however, the activity may or may not constitute a violation of the law, depending on the facts and circumstances involved.

HEALTH CARE CORPORATE COMPLIANCE PROGRAMS

In light of the proliferation of fraud and abuse legislation and enforcement activities directed at the health care industry, it is becoming imperative for health care organizations to implement compliance programs to not only prevent violations but also to reduce the potential for liability should violations occur. Health care providers in all segments of the industry are implementing such programs in response to heightened scrutiny and expectations of compliance but also as part of settlements following health care fraud investigations. The HHS OIG believes that significant reductions in fraud and abuse liability can be accomplished through the use of compliance programs. An effective compliance program can minimize the consequences resulting from a violation of the law and may, in some cases, convince a prosecutor not to pursue a criminal action. With respect to criminal penalties, federal Sentencing Guidelines[193] specifically mandate lesser criminal sanctions for companies that have effective compliance programs in operation. As far as civil sanctions are concerned, the DOJ's Civil Division has implemented a similar philosophy by treating defendants more leniently if they have compliance programs in effect.[194]

In addition to reducing the risk of significant criminal and civil sanctions, a corporate compliance program provides other valuable benefits to health care organizations. A compliance program permits outside counsel to ensure that the organization's documentation and communication procedures make maximum use of the important attorney-client and attorney work-product privileges. Those privileges are among the most important benefits of a well-structured compliance program. A compliance program also establishes a mechanism for employee training on how to handle search warrants and unannounced searches from investigators. Problems such as search warrants, the arrival of investigators at an organization's place of business, and environmental disasters do not allow for a steep learning curve for those involved, and in particular outside legal counsel. Creation of a compliance program establishes a relationship with outside counsel who thereafter is familiar with the company's corporate structure, document system, and general operations. That familiarity will permit prompt, intelligent legal responses to crises that almost always occur without warning. A well-structured compliance program can also reduce the risks of civil suits.

A compliance program establishes a structure to disseminate legal and policy changes quickly and with the confidence that the information will be distributed beyond top management and attorneys. Moreover, an effective compliance program promotes a "law-abiding corporate ethos, and discourages wrongdoing; it provides some protection for officers and directors from individual criminal and civil liability; it affords the opportunity to detect and contain misconduct before it gives rise to civil liability or mushrooms into a full-fledged criminal matter;

and it bestows non-legal benefits such as gaining a reputation for being a good corporate citizen."[195]

Developing a Corporate Compliance Program

Once a health care organization has recognized the need to adopt a corporate compliance program, there are several essential steps that must be followed to implement that goal.

Board Authorization

It is important to understand that a corporate defendant will not be entitled to a fine reduction for having a compliance program unless the program is deemed to be "effective" under the Sentencing Guidelines. The implementation of a compliance program will ultimately determine whether the program is effective within the meaning of the Guidelines. Therefore, a compliance program must be a guide for daily living in the corporation. It cannot be stashed away on a shelf collecting dust, waiting to be pulled out and paraded in front of a federal prosecutor or judge. If the compliance program is in effect a "paper plan," the DOJ will strongly oppose any downward adjustment of a sentence.

Consequently, before a board of directions approves and adopts a compliance program, it must commit itself to spending the time and money needed to carry out the goals set forth in the program. It is crucial to the success and effectiveness of the program that the decision to adopt a corporate compliance program have the full support of the highest level of personnel in a company. This is best accomplished by a formal resolution of the board of directors authorizing the creation and adoption of the compliance program. A formal endorsement by upper management will convey to all employees and, if necessary, to law enforcement officials that the company is fully committed to achieving genuine compliance.

The Legal Audit

The creation of a corporate compliance program begins with a legal audit. A legal audit is a comprehensive study of a company's compliance needs. Any legal audit should begin with an audit plan that includes:

- clearly defined goals that identify the specific company practices to be audited
- the personnel who will conduct the audit
- the individuals to be interviewed
- the documents to be reviewed
- the steps to be taken to ensure protection by the attorney-client privilege

Closely related is the use to which the audit results will be put. An audit should begin with more than just its scope in mind; the audit should have as its final goal the improvement or implementation of a system of self-executing compliance and detection.

To maximize the attorney-related privileges, the audit plan should be carefully structured from the beginning to include a resolution of the board of directors authorizing the audit and spelling out its purposes, including all types of potential litigation. Use of outside counsel to conduct the audit is highly recommended because it will offer additional protection regarding the attorney-related privileges and will lend credibility and independence to the compliance program, which in turn may later persuade the government not to prosecute or at least that the program is genuine.

Before the audit begins, counsel should identify someone from management who is authorized to make interim decisions. This will help speed the process by offering continuity and prompt decision making. The lines of communication should be spelled out before the audit begins. It is common for an audit team to be pressured by everyone concerned to relate information learned during the audit. All information should be kept confidential and disclosed on only a need-to-know basis.

If a compliance program is to be truly effective and comprehensive, the audit process must be as extensive as the intended compliance program. A legal audit includes a review of a company's existing and contemplated business activities; areas of operation that pose a high risk of exposure; any past legal or ethical problems, existing policies, procedures, and compliance efforts; and all laws and regulations applicable to the company's business activities.

As the audit team is put together, two important goals should be kept in mind:

1. To obtain an accurate picture of the company's operation.
2. To preserve the confidentiality of the information.

Thus, the audit should be conducted or at least supervised directly by counsel and preferably outside counsel. A key goal of the audit is honest employee disclosure. If employees disclose past or ongoing wrongdoing, such disclosures can be demanded by government investigators unless protected by the attorney-client privilege. Moreover, employees are likely to be more open with outside counsel. In-house counsel is often viewed as part of management and may well have a chilling effect on the employees being interviewed.

The audit should include interviews with personnel at all levels of the company structure who will best educate the team on the operations of the company. No employee is too high-ranking or too low-level for the audit. Indeed, the audit team should have a healthy skepticism toward high-level personnel who say low-level employees "know the rules and are doing as they are told." Experienced counsel rarely conduct an audit that does not turn up behavior that startles management. Audit interviews should also include "agents" with whom the company subcontracts or to whom it delegates responsibilities.

The legal audit should be a productive and cooperative effort between counsel, management, and employees. Therefore, how the audit is introduced and explained to company personnel is crucial. It is recommended that the explanation come from management and then from legal auditors in a straightforward and honest fashion. The size of the company, the company's established method of internal communication, and the educational makeup of the employees will determine what form the explanation will take (e.g., memos, letters, or meetings). The employees should be told that the audit and future compliance program stem from the company's desire to be a good corporate citizen, to minimize violations of the law, and to take advantage of the benefits of a compliance program.

Employee Interviews

Employees can be a wealth of information concerning company activities, corner-cutting, violations of company policy, and even past or current wrongdoing. Thus, protecting the disclosures made during the audit interviews is crucial. Among the most important considerations for a court determining whether a communication is protected by the attorney-client privilege are:

- the intent of the parties at the time the communication was made
- whether the information was provided by counsel or sought from counsel primarily for the purpose of obtaining legal advice as opposed to obtaining business advice
- whether the subsequent behavior of those claiming the privilege was consistent with that intent and whether any relevant documents were safeguarded.

The first step in preserving the attorney-client privilege protection for the audit process is to create a board resolution or similar document that states:

- the name of the law firm hired or the name of the designated in-house counsel
- that said counsel is to take all steps necessary to acquire information for the purpose of advising the company on the creation of a corporate compliance program

The next step is to ensure that those participating or directly supervising the process are attorneys. Third, all documents produced by counsel and the audit team should be properly labeled as protected by attorney-client privilege and attorney work-product doctrine. Such documents should be disseminated on only a need-to-know basis within the company.

Finally, employee interviews should be structured to maximize the attorney-client privilege. Before an interview begins, the employee should be told the purpose of the interview, who the interviewers are and for whom they work (the company), and that an attorney-client relationship exists between the attorney and the company (not the employee) with respect to what the employee says during the interview. The employee should also be told that the privilege belongs to the company and only the company may choose to waive it. Memoranda of employee interviews should contain verification that the employee was properly informed of the nature of the relationship between counsel and the company.

There always remains a risk that a report by counsel to the company could contain conclusions about an employee's conduct that the employee believes are defamatory, thus leading to new litigation. Such a risk highlights again the importance of using counsel experienced in performing internal investigations.

Mini-Billing Audit

Not every company will be able to expend the funds necessary to commission a corporate compliance program. Many small businesses, from a two-person physician group practice to an ambulance company, are at some risk of being future investigative targets. In lieu of commissioning a full compliance program, some practitioners and providers are opting for a limited legal audit of a particular billing arrangement. The OIG's Operation Restore Trust initiative plainly signals affected providers to review certain billing practices. For instance, the Fraud Alert regarding the way in which ancillary services are provided to nursing facility residents serves as an excellent subject of just such a discreet audit.

The provider should ensure that the counsel who performs the audit is experienced in the reimbursement area as well as in OIG investigations generally. By having an attorney conduct the audit, any findings and recommendations can be protected by the attorney-client privilege. In addition, if the billing practice in question ever becomes the subject of an investigation in the future, then the provider may have an advice of counsel defense, assuming that the provider followed the attorney's recommendations regarding the billing arrangement.

The provider should negotiate with counsel about an estimated cost for this audit. The cost may vary depending on how thorough an audit is desired by the provider. For example, the provider may want counsel to interview all of the individuals involved in supplying and furnishing DME and/or parenteral and enteral supplies to nursing homes. The audit may involve more time if the provider wants a review of practices occurring at more than one facility.

In general, this limited audit involves interviewing the Medicare Part B supply company manger and anyone involved in submitting claims for supply items, as well as possible interviews with the pharmacy that sells the items to the supply company, and a representative of the nursing facility. After conducting the necessary interviews, counsel then prepares a questionnaire regarding any other aspects of billing for these supply items and distributes the survey to the appropriate people at the supplier and the nursing facility. After reviewing the survey responses and the interviews, counsel then can prepare an opinion letter setting forth the facts, the applicable law (such as the fraud and abuse statutes as well as the Medicare supplier regulations), and provide an analysis of the degree of risk posed by the current arrangement under those provisions.

The provider greatly values this outside audit, as it permits the supplier and the facility to review the existing billing practices and revise these practices, if necessary. Also, it can ensure that the proper agreements are in place and that residents are receiving necessary information regarding the supplies that are furnished to them.

There are any number of different billing practices that could be reviewed using this vehicle. However, the mini-audit may be of greatest interest to those providers who are the focus of Operation Restore Trust. For example, a home health agency may want to review the way in which it assists in the discharge planning process at area hospitals or its cost reporting practices.

Program Design

A compliance and detection program should be designed in part with its final critics in mind: the public, stockholders, and often the government. Among the most important components in the design of any program are the Guidelines. The Guidelines themselves spell out a useful starting point by describing "seven minimum steps" that a compliance program must include, with the precise actions necessary to implement those steps dependent on the size of the organization, the nature of its business, and its history.

Section 8A1.3.(k) of the Guidelines provide that an "effective" compliance program must be "reasonably designed, implemented, and enforced so that it generally will be effective in preventing and detecting criminal conduct." The "hallmark" of an effective program is that the company takes measures to prevent criminal and other wrongful conduct by its employees and other agents. "Due diligence requires at a minimum that the organization must have taken the following types of steps:"

First, the company must establish compliance standards and procedures to be followed by its employees and other agents that are reasonably capable of reducing the prospect of criminal or wrongful conduct.

Second, an effective compliance program must address oversight responsibilities. Specifically, the company must assign individuals in high-level personnel positions with the overall responsibility to oversee compliance with the standards and procedures that will be developed after the legal audit is completed.

Third, in accomplishing the above requirement, the company must use due care not to delegate substantial discretionary authority to individuals whom the organization knew, or should have known through the exercise of due diligence, had a propensity to engage in illegal activities.

Fourth, the Guidelines require that once suitable standards and procedures are developed, the company must take steps to communicate effectively its standards and procedures to all employees and other agents. The company will be required to develop and implement adequate training programs for its employees that explain in a practical manner what is required.

Fifth, the Guidelines further require that the company develop a monitoring and auditing system reasonably designed to detect criminal and other wrongful conduct by its employees and other agents. An adequate monitoring and auditing system will satisfy the required element under the Guidelines that the company take reasonable steps to achieve compliance with its standards. Pursuant to this requirement, the company must also have in place and publicize a reporting system whereby employees and other agents can report criminal and other wrongful conduct by others within the company without fear of retribution.

Sixth, once a company has established compliance standards and procedures, the Guidelines require that a company implement an adequate enforcement and discipline procedure that will ensure consistent enforcement of the compliance standards via an appropriate disciplinary mechanism. The enforcement and discipline mechanism must also provide adequate discipline of individuals responsible for "failing to detect an offense." Adequate discipline of individuals responsible for an offense is also a necessary component of enforcement. The form of appropriate discipline, however, will be case specific.

The final element of an effective compliance program requires the company to take all reasonable steps to respond to a detected offense and to prevent further similar offenses, including any necessary modifications to its program.

NOTES

1. Pub. L. No. 104-191.

2. *See* Bureau of National Affairs, *FBI Funding to Target Fraud and Abuse Increased by Health Insurance Reform Law*, 1 HEALTH CARE FRAUD REPORT no. 2, Jan. 29, 1997, at 43.

3. *See* United States v. CMS Management-Tucker Inc., No. 96-1271, *consent order entered* (E.D. Pa. Feb. 21, 1996).

4. *See* Bureau of National Affairs, *Justice Aims to Increase Prosecutors, Focus on Managed Care, Quality of Care*, 1 HEALTH CARE FRAUD REPORT no. 1, Jan. 15, 1997, at 8.

5. *See* Pogue v. American Healthcare, 914 F. Supp. 1507 (M.D. Tenn. 1996).

6. *See Health Care Leaders Say Care Givers are "Under Siege" by Federal Investigators*, TODAY'S NEWS, July 10, 1997.

7. 42. U.S.C. § 1320a-7a.

8. 31 U.S.C. §§ 3729 through 3733.

9. 42 U.S.C. § 1395nn.

10. Pub. L. No. 104-191.

11. *See* United States v. Hershenow, 680 F.2d 847 (1st. Cir. 1982).

12. People v. American Med. Ctrs., 324 N.W.2d 782 (Mich. Ct. App. 1982), *cert. denied*, 464 U.S. 1009 (1983).

13. Pub. L. No. 104-191, to be codified at 42 U.S.C. § 1320a-7a(a)(1).

14. *See* Bureau of National Affairs, AHA, *Ohio Hospitals Sue Government to Stop False Claims Act Abuse*, HEALTH LAW REPORTER vol. 5, Oct. 10, 1996, at 1479.

15. 42 U.S.C. § 1395ww(a)(4).

16. This legislative enactment was implemented in an interim final regulation published at 59 Fed. Reg. 1,654 (1994), codified at 42 C.F.R. § 412.2(c)(5).

17. 42 U.S.C. §§ 1395e & 1395l.

18. *See* Department of Health & Human Services, Office of Inspector General, Special Fraud Alert: OIG Announcement 91-23 (1991).

19. Pub. L. No. 104-191, to be codified at 42 U.S.C. § 1320a-7a.

20. Joint Explanatory Statement on H.R. Doc. No. 104-736 3103, Health Insurance Portability and Accountability Act of 1996, 104 Cong., 2d Sess. (1996).

21. Medicare Intermediary Manual § 3951.

22. 42 U.S.C. § 1320a-7b.

23. 59 Fed. Reg. 61,571 (1994).

24. 42 U.S.C. § 1395mm(i)(6) & 42 C.F.R. § 1003.103(f).

25. 61 Fed. Reg. 13,430 (1996), to be codified at 42 C.F.R. Part 1003.

26. Pub. L. No. 104-191, to be codified at 42 U.S.C. § 1320a-7a.

27. 42 U.S.C. § 1395mm(i)(8).

28. 42 U.S.C. § 1320a-7b.

29. United States v. Greber, 760 F.2d 68 (3d Cir.), *cert. denied*, 474 U.S. 988 (1985).

30. United States v. Greber, 760 F.2d 68 (3d Cir.), *cert. denied*, 474 U.S. 988 (1985).

31. United States v. Kats, 871 F.2d 105 (9th Cir. 1989).

32. United States v. Bay State Ambulance & Hosp. Rental Serv., 874 F.2d 20 (1st Cir. 1989).

33. Department of Health & Human Services, Office of Inspector General, Special Fraud Alert on Joint Venture Arrangements, OIG-89-04 (Apr. 1989).

34. *See* Inspector Gen. v. Hanlester Network, Docket No. C-448, Decision No. 1347, HHS Departmental Appeals Board, Appellate Division (July 24, 1992), *aff'd sub nom.* Hanlester Network v. Sullivan, No. CF-92-4552-LHM (C.D. Cal. Feb. 10, 1993).

35. Hanlester Network v. Shalala, No. 93-55351 (9th Cir. Apr. 6, 1995) (unpublished).

36. Department of Health and Human Services, Office of Inspector General, Oct. 1991.

37. Department of Health & Human Services, Special Fraud Alert: Hospital Incentives to Physicians (May 7, 1992).

38. Polk County Mem'l Hosp. v. Peters, 800 F. Supp. 1451 (E.D. Tex. 1992).

39. *See also* Vana Vista Hosp. Sys. Inc., No., 233623 (Cal. Super. Ct. Riverside County, Oct. 25, 1993) (unpublished).

40. Letter from D. McCarthy Thornton, Associate General Counsel of Health and Human Services, Office of Inspector General to the I.R.S. Office of Associate Chief Counsel, Dec. 22, 1992.

41. *See* IRS Exemption Letter to Facey Medical Foundation, Mar. 31, 1993, in which the IRS stated "We express no opinion as to whether the planned purchase of the stock of a private group medical practice by your affiliate or your subsequent purchase of services from that group practice for a percentage of your gross revenues complies with these (federal antikickback) provisions."

42. Pub. L. No. 104-191, to be codified at 42 U.S.C. § 1320a-7b.

43. HHS issued a final interim regulation addressing procedures for presenting requests for advisory opinions, 62 Fed. Reg. 7,350 (1997), to be codified at 42 C.F.R. part 1008. The rule specifies that an advisory opinion will not be issued if a request presents a general question of interpretation or a hypothetical situation, if it does not relate to a named individual or entity, if the same or similar course of action is already under investigation by a government agency, or if an informed opinion cannot be made without an extensive investigation or clinical study.

44. Reprinted with adaptations and revisions from Jennifer A. Stiller, Rosemary L. Auth, and Lynn A. Powe, *Third Party Payer Considerations*, in Hospital Contracts Manual, Baker & Hostetler © 1993, Aspen Publishers, Inc.

45. 42 U.S.C. § 1320a-7b.

46. 56 Fed. Reg. 35,952 (1991), to be codified at 42 C.F.R. § 1001.952.

47. 57 Fed. Reg. 3,330 (1992), as amended 57 Fed. Reg. 52,729 (1992), to be codified at 42 C.F.R. § 1001.952.

48. 58 Fed. Reg. 49,008 (1993), to be codified at 42 C.F.R. § 1001.952.

49. 59 Fed. Reg. 37,202 (1994), to be codified at § 1001.952.

50. Pub. L. No. 104-191, to be codified at 42 U.S.C. § 1320a-7b.

51. 42 C.F.R. § 1001.952.

52. 42 C.F.R. § 1001.952(a)(1).

53. 42 C.F.R. § 1001.954(a)(2).

54. 42 C.F.R. § 1001.952(b).

55. 42 C.F.R. § 1001.952(c).

56. 42 C.F.R. § 1001.952(d).

57. 42 C.F.R. § 1001.952(e).

58. 42 C.F.R. § 1001.952(f).

59. 42 C.F.R. § 1001.952(g).

60. That definition (at 15 U.S.C. § 2301(6)) provides:

The term "written warranty" means—

(A) any written affirmation of fact or written promise made in connection with the sale of a consumer product by a supplier to a buyer which relates to the nature of the material or workmanship and affirms or promises that such material or workmanship is defect free or will meet a specified level of performance over a specified period of time, or

(B) any undertaking in writing in connection with the sale by a supplier of a consumer product to refund, repair, replace, or take other remedial action with respect to such product in the event that such product fails to meet the specifications set forth in the undertaking, which written affirmation, promise, or undertaking becomes part of the basis of the bargain between a supplier and a buyer for purposes other than resale of such product.

61. 42 C.F.R. § 1001.952(h).

62. 42 C.F.R. § 1001.952(i).

63. *see* 26 U.S.C. § 3121(d)(2).

64. 42 C.F.R. § 1001.952(j).

65. 42 C.F.R. § 1001.952(k).

66. 57 Fed. Reg. 52,723 (1992), codified at 42 C.F.R. § 1001.952.

67. 57 Fed. Reg. 52,723 (1992), codified at 42 C.F.R. § 1001.952.

68. 42 C.F.R. § 1001.952(1).

69. 42 C.F.R. § 1001.952(m).

70. Pub. L. No. 104-191, to be codified at 42 U.S.C. § 1320a-7b(B)(3).

71. Pub. L. No. 104-191.

72. 42 U.S.C. § 1320a-7b.

73. 42 U.S.C. § 1320a-7b(a)(1).

74. "Federal health care programs" is defined as any plan or program that provides health benefits, directly through insurance or otherwise, that is funded in whole or in part by the federal government. Pub. L. No. 104-191, to be codified at 42 U.S.C. § 1320a-7b.

75. 42 U.S.C. §§ 1320a-7b(a)(2-5) & 1320a-7b(c).

76. 18 U.S.C. § 287. The statute states:

Whoever makes or presents to any person or officer in the civil, military, or naval service of the United States, or any department or agency thereof, any claim upon or against the United States, or any department or agency thereof, knowing such claim to be false, fictitious, or fraudulent, shall be imprisoned not more than five years and shall be subject to a fine in the amount provided in this title.

77. *See* United States v. Catena, 500 F.2d at 1319 (3d. Cir. 1974) (holding the defendant-physician liable under § 287 on the theory that he caused the insurer to submit the false claim to the government).

78. Pub. L. No. 95-142, codified at 42 U.S.C. § 1320a-7b.

79. United States v. Greber, 760 F.2d 68 (3d Cir.), *cert denied,* 474 U.S. 988 (1985).

80. United States v. Kats, 871 F.2d 105 (9th Cir. 1989).

81. Pub. L. No. 104-191, to be codified at 18 U.S.C. §§ 669, 1035, 1347 and 1518.

82. Pub. L. No. 104-191, § 241(b), to be codified at 18 U.S.C. ch. 1.

83. *See, e.g.,* United States v. Lorenzo, 768 F. Supp. 1127 (E.D. Pa. 1991) (assessing civil penalties totaling $18.4 million against a physician found guilty of filing 3,683 false Medicare claims).

84. 42 U.S.C. § 1320a-7a.

85. Pub. L. No. 104-91, to be codified at 42 U.S.C. § 1320a-7a.

86. Pub. L. No. 104-91, to be codified at 42 U.S.C. § 1320a-7a(1).

87. 42 U.S.C. § 1320a-7a.

88. 42 U.S.C. § 1320a-7a(I)(3)(B).

89. 42 U.S.C. § 1320a-7a(I)(3)(A).

90. H.R. Rep. No. 391, 100th Cong., 1st Sess., pt. 1, at 534 (1987). Note that the HIPAA provides a definition for the term "should know," as acting in deliberate ignorance with respect to the information, or in reckless disregard of the truth or falsity of the information.

91. Pub. L. No. 104-191, to be codified at 42 U.S.C. § 1320a-7a(1).

92. 42 U.S.C. § 1320a-7a(d).

93. 42 U.S.C. § 1320a-7a(e).

94. 42 U.S.C. § 1320a-7a(c)(1).

95. 42 U.S.C. § 1320a-7a(k).

96. 42 U.S.C. § 1320a-7a(c)(3).

97. Scott v. Bowen, 845 F.2d 856 (9th Cir. 1988).

98. Mayers v. U.S. Dep't of Health & Human Servs., 806 F.2d 995 (11th Cir.), *cert. denied,* 484 U.S. 822 (1986).

99. *See, e.g.,* Chapman v. U.S. Dep't of Health & Human Servs., 821 F.2d 523 (10th Cir. 1987) (civil penalties of $156,318 for filing 19 false Medicaid claims justified); Mayers v. U.S. Dep't of Health & Human Servs., 806 F.2d 995 (11th Cir.), *cert. denied,* 484 U.S. 822 (1986) (civil penalties of $1,791,100 for filing 2,702 false Medicare claims justified).

100. Pub. L. No. 104-191, to be codified at 42 U.S.C. § 1320a-7a.

101. Bernstein v. Sullivan, 914 F.2d 1395 (10th Cir. 1990).

102. Mayers v. U.S. Dep't of Health & Human Servs., 806 F.2d 995 (11th Cir.), *cert. denied,* 484 U.S. 822 (1986).

103. 31 U.S.C. §§ 3729 through 3733.

104. *See* Francis J. Serbaroli, *Provider Liabilities under the False Claims Act,* N.Y.L.J. 3 (1994), for discussion.

105. United States v. Halper, 490 U.S. 435 (1989).

106. United States v. Halper, 490 U.S. 435 (1989).

107. United States v. Pani, 717 F. Supp. 1013 (S.D.N.Y. 1989).

108. *See also* Greene v. Sullivan, 731 F. Supp. 835 (E.D. Tenn. 1990); Manocchio v. Kusserow, 961 F.2d 1539 (11th Cir. 1992).

109. 31 U.S.C. § 3729(a).

110. *See, e.g.,* Hagood v. Sonoma County Water Agency, 929 F.2d 1416 (9th Cir. 1991); United States v. Kensington Hosp., 760 F. Supp. 1120 (E.D. Pa. 1991).

111. 31 U.S.C. § 3729(b). These broad definitions were made a part of the 1986 amendments to clarify prior law and to avoid decisions such as *United States v. Ueber,* 299 F.2d 310 (6th Cir. 1962), which required actual knowledge. *See* The False Claims Reform Act of 1985, S. Rep. No. 345, 99th Cong., 2d Sess. 2, at 7.

112. 31 U.S.C. § 3729(b).

113. United States v. Oakwood Downriver Med. Ctr., 687 F. Supp. 302 (E.D. Mich. 1988). *See also* United States v. Children's Shelter, Inc., 604 F. Supp. 865 (C.D. Okla. 1985).

114. Hagood v. Sonoma County Water Agency, 929 F.2d 1416 (9th Cir. 1991).

115. Wang v. FMC Corp., 975 F.2d 1412 (9th Cir. 1992).

116. Francis J. Serbaroli, *Provider Liabilities under the False Claims Act,* N.Y.L.J. 3 (1994).

117. The term "qui tam" is derived from the phrase, *"qui tam pro domino rege quam pro se ipso in hac parte sequitur,"* meaning "he who brings the action

for the king as well as for himself." Blackstone, Commentaries on the Law of England, Book III, 160 (1768).

118. 31 U.S.C. § 3731(b).

119. Francis J. Serbaroli, *Provider Liabilities under the False Claims Act,* N.Y.L.J. 3 (1994).

120. United States v. NEC Corp., 11 F.3d 136 (11th Cir. 1993).

121. United States v. NEC Corp., 11 F.3d 136 (11th Cir. 1993).

122. 31 U.S.C. § 3730(a-b).

123. 31 U.S.C. § 3731(b).

124. 41 U.S.C. §§ 51 through 56.

125. United States v. Kensington Hosp., 700 F. Supp. 1120 (E.D. Pa. 1991).

126. Roy v. Anthony, 914 F. Supp. 1504 (S.D. Ohio 1994).

127. Pogue v. American Healthcorp, 914 F. Supp. 1507 (M.D. Tenn. 1996).

128. Pub. L. No. 100-93, to be codified at 42 U.S.C. § 1320a-7.

129. Pub. L. No. 104-191, to be codified at 42 U.S.C. § 1320a-7.

130. *See* Thorbus v. Bowen, 848 F.2d 901 (8th Cir. 1988).

131. 42 C.F.R. § 1001.102.

132. 42 C.F.R. § 1001.201.

133. 42 C.F.R. § 1001.301.

134. 42 C.F.R. § 1001.601.

135. 42 C.F.R. § 1001.701. Note that the HIPAA changes these sanctions against providers who fail to fulfill their statutory obligations (by failing to meet professionally recognized standards or providing unnecessary items and services) in that the statute establishes a minimum one-year exclusion period. The statute also abrogates the requirement that the Secretary establish that the provider was "unwilling or unable" to meet statutory obligations before imposing exclusion as a sanction.

136. 42 C.F.R. § 1001.901.

137. 42 C.F.R. § 1001.951.

138. 42 C.F.R. § 1001.952. Note that under the HIPAA, individuals with a direct or indirect ownership interest in a sanctioned entity or the managing officers of such an entity may be sanctioned without the government having to offer evidence of their personal wrongdoing. The government will have to demonstrate that investors acted in deliberate indifference to the information. With respect to officers and managing employees of an organization, however, sanctions are possible even if there is no evidence that they had knowledge or otherwise participated in the wrongful activities.

139. 42 C.F.R. § 1001.1101.

140. Pub. L. No. 104-191, to be codified at 42 U.S.C. § 1320a-7.

141. 42 C.F.R. § 1001.1901(b)(1).

142. *See, e.g.,* 42 C.F.R. § 1001.1901.

143. 42 C.F.R. § 1001.301(a).

144. 42 C.F.R. § 1001.3001 (a)(3).

145. 42 C.F.R. § 001.3004(c).

146. 42 C.F.R. § 405.370.

147. 42 C.F.R. § 405.371(a).
148. 42 C.F.R. § 405.371(b).
149. 42 C.F.R. § 405.373(c).
150. 42 U.S.C. § 1395nn.
151. 42 U.S.C. § 1395nn(a). The prohibition in Stark I therefore applies only to clinical laboratory services, ordered by a physician for a Medicare patient. Stark II considerably expands the scope of the prohibition on physician self-referral, as is discussed later in this section.
152. 42 U.S.C. § 1395nn(g).
153. 60 Fed. Reg. 41,914 (1995), to be codified at 42 C.F.R. 411350 through 411.361.
154. 42 U.S.C. § 1395nn(h)(5)(A).
155. 42 U.S.C. § 1395nn(h)(5)(c).
156. In the version of Stark II that was enacted in August 1993, the definition included radiology or other diagnostic services. In a bill approved by the House and Senate on October 8, 1994, H.B. No. 5252, the reference to "other diagnostic services" was deleted, and the above wording added.
157. 42 U.S.C. § 1395nn(h)(6).
158. 42 U.S.C. § 1395nn(h)(6).
159. 42 U.S.C. § 1395nn(h)(1).
160. 42 U.S.C. § 1395nn(h)(1)(C)(I).
161. 60 Fed. Reg. 41,914 (1995), codified at 42 C.F.R. § 411.350.
162. *See* John Steiner, *Update: Fraud and Abuse and Stark Laws,* 9 J. Health & Hosp. L. 26 (1993).
163. "Group practice" is defined at § 1395nn(h)(4) of the law and is discussed in Definition of "Group Practice."
164. 42 U.S.C. § 1395nn(b)(1).
165. 42 U.S.C. § 1395nn(b)(1).
166. 42 U.S.C. § 1395nn(b)(2)(A).
167. 60 Fed. Reg. 41,914 (1995), codified at 42 C.F.R. § 411.350.
168. 60 Fed. Reg. 41,914 (1995), codified at 42 C.F.R. § 411.350.
169. 60 Fed. Reg. 41,914 (1995), codified at 42 C.F.R. § 411.350.
170. 42 U.S.C. § 1395nn(h)(4)(A).
171. 42 U.S.C. § 1395nn(h)(4)(B).
172. Medicare Program; Physician Self-Referral Regulations: Change in Date for Submission of Group Attestation Statement, 60 Fed. Reg. 63,438 (1995), codified at 42 C.F.R. pt. 411.
173. *See* The Health Maintenance Organization Act of 1973, 42 U.S.C. § 300e.
174. 42 U.S.C. § 1395nn(c).
175. 42 U.S.C. § 1395nn(d)(3).
176. 42 U.S.C. § 1395nn(d)(2)(D).
177. 42 U.S.C. § 1395nn(d)(2).
178. 42 U.S.C. § 1395nn(d)(1).
179. 42 U.S.C. § 1395nn(e)(1).
180. 42 U.S.C. § 1395nn(e)(2).

181. 42 U.S.C. § 1395nn(e)(3).

182. 42 U.S.C. § 1395nn(e)(B)(ii).

183. 42 U.S.C. § 1395nn(e)(B)(i).

184. 42 U.S.C. § 1395nn(e)(4).

185. 42 U.S.C. § 1395nn(e)(5).

186. 42 U.S.C. § 1395nn(e)(6).

187. 60 Fed. Reg. 41,914 (1995), codified at 42 C.F.R. § 411.350.

188. 42 U.S.C. § 1395nn(e)(7).

189. 42 U.S.C. § 1395nn(e)(8).

190. 42 U.S.C. § 1395nn(h)(1)(c).

191. 42 C.F.R. § 411.361. Note that HHS delayed enforcement of the reporting requirements established under Stark II. According to a letter signed by June Gibbs Brown, HHS Inspector General, and HCFA Administrator Bruce Vladeck, addressed to the General Counsel for the American Hospital Association, providers will not be held to the reporting requirements under § 1877(f) until a proper form and accompanying booklet are developed and issued.

192. 42 U.S.C. § 1395nn(g).

193. United States Sentencing Commission Guidelines, Sentencing for Organizations, 56 Fed. Reg. 22,762 (1991).

194. Arent et al., Health Law Trends, The Dawning of the Age of Compliance, vol. 1, 1996.

195. Barr & Weinreich, *The Science of Compliance,* Int'l Fin. Rev. (Sept. 1993).

Fraud Alerts and Other Administrative Guidance

SPECIAL FRAUD ALERT: ROUTINE WAIVER OF COPAYMENTS OR DEDUCTIBLES UNDER MEDICARE PART B

The Office of Inspector General was established at the Department of Health and Human Services by Congress in 1976 to identify and eliminate fraud, abuse, and waste in Health and Human Services programs and to promote efficiency and economy in departmental operations. It carries out this mission through a nationwide network of audits, investigations, and inspections. To help reduce fraud in the Medicare program, the Office of Inspector General is actively investigating health care providers, practitioners, and suppliers of health care items and services who (1) are paid on the basis of charges[1] and (2) routinely waive (do not bill) Medicare deductible and copayment charges to beneficiaries for items and services covered by the Medicare program.

Source: Reprinted from Department of Health & Human Services, Office of Inspector General, *Special Fraud Alert: Routine Waiver of Copayments or Deductibles under Medicaid Part B.* OIG-91-23.

What Are Medicare Deductible and Copayment Charges?

The Medicare "deductible" is the amount that must be paid by a Medicare beneficiary before Medicare will pay for any items or services for that individual. Currently, the Medicare Part B deductible is $100 per year.

"Copayment" (or "coinsurance") is the portion of the cost of an item or service that the Medicare beneficiary must pay. Currently, Medicare Part B coinsurance is generally 20 percent of the reasonable charge for the item or service. Typically, if the Medicare reasonable charge for a Part B item or service is $100, the Medicare beneficiary (who has met his or her deductible) must pay $20 of the physician's bill, and Medicare will pay $80.

Why Is It Illegal for "Charge-Based" Providers, Practitioners, and Suppliers to Routinely Waive Medicare Copayment and Deductibles?

Routine waiver of deductibles and copayments by charge-based providers, practitioners, or suppliers is unlawful because it results in (1) false claims, (2) violations of the antikickback statute, and (3) excessive utilization of items and services paid for by Medicare.

A "charge-based" provider, practitioner, or supplier is one who is paid by Medicare on the basis of the "reasonable charge" for the item or service provided. 42 U.S.C. § 1395u(b)(3); 42 C.F.R. 405.501. Medicare typically pays 80 percent of the reasonable charge. 42 U.S.C. § 1395l(a)(1). The criteria for determining what charges are reasonable are contained in regulations, and include examination of (1) the actual charge for the item or service, (2) the customary charge for similar items or services, and (3) the prevailing charge in the same locality for similar items or services. The Medicare reasonable charge can exceed the actual charge for the item or service, and may generally not exceed the customary charge or the highest prevailing charge for the item or service. In some cases the provider, practitioner, or supplier will be paid the lesser of the actual charge or an amount established by a fee schedule.

A provider, practitioner, or supplier who routinely waives Medicare copayments or deductibles is misstating the actual charge. For example, if a supplier claims that the charge for a piece of equipment is $100, but routinely waives the copayment, the actual charge is $80. Medicare should be paying 80 percent of $80 (or $64), rather than 80 percent of $100 (or $80). As a result of the supplier's misrepresentation, the Medicare program is paying $16 more than it should for this item.

In certain cases, a provider, practitioner, or supplier that routinely waives Medicare copayments or deductibles also could be held liable under the Medicare and Medicaid antikickback statute, 42 U.S.C. § 1320a-7b(b). This statute makes it illegal to offer, pay, solicit, or receive anything of value as an inducement to generate business payable by Medicare or Medicaid. When providers, practitioners, or suppliers forgive financial obligations for reasons other than genuine financial hardship of the particular patient, they may be unlawfully inducing that patient to purchase items or services from them.

At first glance, it may appear that routine waiver of copayments and deductibles helps Medicare beneficiaries. By waiving Medicare copayments and deductibles, the provider of services may claim that the beneficiary incurs no costs. In fact, this is not true. Studies have shown that if patients are required to pay even a small portion of their care, they will be better health care consumers, and select items or services because they are medically needed, rather than simply because they are free. Ultimately, if Medicare pays more for an item or service than it should, or if it pays for unnecessary items or services, there are fewer Medicare funds available to pay for truly needed services.

One important exception to the prohibition against waiving copayments and deductibles is that providers, practitioners, or suppliers may forgive the copayment in consideration of a particular patient's financial hardship. This hardship exception, however, must not be used routinely; it should be used occasionally to address the special financial needs of a particular patient. Except in such special cases, a good-faith effort to collect deductibles and copayments must be made. Otherwise, claims submitted to Medicare may violate the statutes discussed above and other provisions of the law.

What Penalties Can Someone Be Subject to for Routinely Waiving Medicare Copayments or Deductibles?

Whoever submits a false claim to the Medicare program (for example, a claim misrepresents an actual charge) may be subject to criminal, civil, or administrative liability for making false statements and/or submitting false claims to the Government. 18 U.S.C. §§ 287 & 1001; 31 U.S.C. § 3729; 42 U.S.C. § 1320a-7. Penalties can include imprisonment, criminal fines, civil damages and forfeitures, civil monetary penalties, and exclusion from Medicare and the State health care programs.

In addition, anyone who routinely waives copayments or deductibles can be criminally prosecuted under 42 U.S.C. § 1320a-7b(b), and excluded from participating in Medicare and the State health care programs under the antikickback statute. 42 U.S.C. § 1320a-7(b)(7).

Finally, anyone who furnishes items or services to patients substantially in excess of the needs of such patients can be excluded from Medicare and the State health care programs. 42 U.S.C. § 1320a-7(b)(6)(B).

Indications of Improper Waiver of Deductibles and Copayments

To help you identify charge-based providers, practitioners, or suppliers who routinely waive Medicare deductibles and copayments, listed below are some suspect marketing practices. Please note that this list is not intended to be exhaustive but, rather, to highlight some indicators of potentially unlawful activity.

- Advertisements that state: "Medicare Accepted As Payment In Full," "Insurance Accepted As Payment In Full," or "No Out-of-Pocket Expense."
- Advertisements that promise that "discounts" will be given to Medicare beneficiaries.
- Routine use of "Financial hardship" forms that state that the beneficiary is unable to pay the coinsurance/deductible

(i.e., there is no good-faith attempt to determine the beneficiary's actual financial condition).

- Collection of copayments and deductibles only when the beneficiary has Medicare supplemental insurance ("Medigap") coverage (i.e., the items or services are "free" to the beneficiary).
- Charges to Medicare beneficiaries that are higher than those made to other persons for similar services and items (the higher charges offset the waiver of coinsurance).
- Failure to collect copayments or deductibles for a specific group of Medicare patients for reasons unrelated to indigency (e.g., a supplier waives coinsurance or deductible for all patients from a particular hospital, in order to get referrals).
- "Insurance programs" that cover copayments or deductibles only for items or services provided by the entity offering the insurance. The "insurance premium" paid by the beneficiary is insignificant and can be as low as $1 a month or even $1 a year. These premiums are not based upon actuarial risks, but instead are a sham used to disguise the routine waiver of copayments and deductibles.

What To Do if You Have Information About Suppliers, Physicians, or Other Providers Who Waive Copayments or Deductibles

If you have information about a provider, practitioner, or supplier who is routinely waiving the Medicare copayment or deductible, contact any regional office of the Office of Investigations in the Department of Health and Human Services at the following locations:

Regions	States Serviced	Telephone
Boston	MA, VT, NH, ME, RI, CT	(617) 565-2660
New York	NY, NJ, PR, VI	(212) 264-1691

Regions	States Serviced	Telephone
Philadelphia	PA, MD, DE, WV, VA	(215) 596-6796
Atlanta	KY, GA, NC, SC, FL, TN, AL, MS	(404) 331-2131
Chicago	IL, MN, WI, MI, IN, OH	(312) 353-2740
Dallas	TX, NM, OK, AR, LA	(214) 767-8406
Kansas City	MO, KS	(816) 426-3811
Denver	CO, UT, WY, MT, ND, SD, IA, NE	(303) 844-5621
San Francisco	CA, NV, AZ, HI	(415) 556-8880
Seattle	WA, OR, ID, AK	(206) 442-0229
Washington, DC	DC & Metrop. areas of VA, MD	(202) 619-1900

If there are special circumstances that make it inconvenient for you to contact one of the regional offices, you may report suspected violations to the Office of Inspector General Hotline. You need not give your name. Written reports are preferred. The Office of Inspector General Hotline address and telephone numbers are:

HHS OIG HOTLINE
Post Office Box 17303
Department of Health & Human Services
Baltimore, Maryland 21203-7303
(301) 965-5953
(FTS) 625-5953
(800) 368-5779 (Toll Free Nationwide)
(800) 638-3986 (Toll Free Maryland Only)

SPECIAL FRAUD ALERT: JOINT VENTURE ARRANGEMENTS

Special Fraud Alert

The Office of Inspector General was established at the Department of Health and Human Services by Congress in 1976 to identity and eliminate fraud, abuse, and waste in Health and Human Services programs and to promote efficiency and economy in departmental operations. It carries out this mission through a nationwide network of audits, investigations, and

---

Source: Reprinted from Department of Health & Human Services, Office of Inspector General, *Special Fraud Alert: Joint Venture Arrangements,* OIG-89-04.

inspections. To help reduce fraud in the Medicare programs, the Office of Inspector General is actively investigating violations of the Medicare and Medicaid antikickback statute, 42 U.S.C. § 1320a-7b(b). This statute is very broad. Among other things, it penalizes anyone who knowingly and willfully solicits, receives, offers, or pays anything of value to induce or in return for:

1. referring an individual to a person for the furnishing or arranging for the furnishing of any item or service payable under the Medicare or Medicaid program, or
2. purchasing, leasing, or ordering, or arranging for or recommending, purchasing, leasing, or ordering any good, facility, service, or item payable under the Medicare or Medicaid programs.

Violations are subject to criminal penalties, or exclusion from participation in the Medicare and Medicaid programs, or both.

The Office of Inspector General has become aware of a proliferation of arrangements between those in a position to refer business, such as physicians, and those providing items or services for which Medicare or Medicaid pays. Some examples of the items or services provided in these arrangements include clinical diagnostic laboratory services, durable medical equipment (DME), and other diagnostic services. Sometimes these deals are called "joint ventures." A joint venture may take a variety of forms: it may be a contractual agreement between two or more parties to cooperate in providing services, or it may involve the creation of a new legal entity by the parties, such as a limited partnership or closely held corporation, to provide such services. Of course, there may be legitimate reasons to form a joint venture, such as raising necessary investment capital. However, the Office of Inspector General believes that some of these joint ventures may violate the Medicare and Medicaid antikickback statute.

Under these suspect joint ventures, physicians may become investors in a newly formed joint venture entity. The investors refer their patients to this new entity, and are paid by the entity in the form of "profit distributions." These suspect joint ventures may be intended not so much to raise investment capital legitimately to start a business, but to lock up a stream of referrals from the physician investors and to compensate them indirectly for these referrals. Because physician investors can benefit financially from their referrals, unnecessary procedures and tests may be ordered or performed, resulting in unnecessary program expenditures.

The questionable features of these suspect joint ventures may be reflected in three areas:

1. the manner in which investors are selected and retained;
2. the nature of the business structure of the joint venture; and
3. the financing and profit distributions.

Suspect Joint Ventures: What To Look For

To help you identify these suspect joint ventures, the following are examples of questionable features, which separately or taken together may result in a business arrangement that violates the antikickback statute. Please note that this is not intended as an exhaustive list, but rather gives examples of indicators of potentially unlawful activity.

Investors

- Investors are chosen because they are in a position to make referrals.
- Physicians who are expected to make a large number of referrals may be offered a greater investment opportunity in the joint venture than those anticipated to make fewer referrals.
- Physician investors may be actively encouraged to make referrals to the joint venture, and may be encouraged to divest their ownership interest if they fail to sustain an "acceptable" level of referrals.
- The joint venture tracks it sources of referrals, and distributes this information to the investors.
- Investors may be required to divest their ownership interest if they cease to practice in the service area, for example, if they move, become disabled, or retire.
- Investment interests may be nontransferable.

Business Structure

- The structure of some joint ventures may be suspect. For example, one of the parties may be an ongoing entity already engaged in a particular line of business. That party may act as the reference laboratory or DME supplier for the joint venture. In some of these cases, the joint venture can be best characterized as a "shell."
- In the case of a shell laboratory joint venture, for example:
    — It conducts very little testing on the premises, even though it is Medicare certified.
    — The reference laboratory may do the vast bulk of the testing at its central processing laboratory, even though it also serves as the "manager" of the shell laboratory.
    — Despite the location of the actual testing, the local "shell" laboratory bills Medicare directly for these tests.
- In the case of a shell DME joint venture, for example:
    — It owns very little of the DME or other capital equipment; rather than ongoing entity owns them.
    — The ongoing entity is responsible for all day-to-day operations of the joint venture, such as delivery of the DME and billing.

Financing and Profit Distributions

- The amount of capital invested by the physician may be disproportionately small and the returns on investment may be disproportionately large when compared to a typical investment in a new business enterprise.
- Physician investors may invest only a nominal amount, such as $500 to $1,500.
- Physician investors may be permitted to "borrow" the amount of the "investment" from the entity, and pay it back through deductions from profit distributions, thus eliminating even the need to contribute cash to the partnership.
- Investors may be paid extraordinary returns on the investment in comparison with the risk involved, often well over 50 percent to 100 percent per year.

What To Do If You Have Information on a Joint Venture That Fits These Features

If you have information on the existence of a joint venture that contains some or all of the features described above, contact the Inspector General Hotline or any of the regional offices of the Office of Inspector General of the Department of Health and Human Services at the following locations:

Regions	States Serviced	Telephone
Boston	MA, VT, NH, ME, RI, CT	(617) 565-2660
New York	NY, NJ, PR, VI	(212) 264-1691
Philadelphia	PA, MD, DE, WV, VA	(215) 596-6796
Atlanta	KY, GA, NC, SC, FL, TN, AL, MS	(404) 331-2131
Chicago	IL, MN, WI, MI, IN, OH	(312) 353-2740
Dallas	TX, NM, OK, AR, LA	(214) 767-8406
Kansas City	MO, KS	(816) 426-3811
Denver	CO, UT, WY, MT, ND, SD, IA, NE	(303) 844-5621
San Francisco	CA, NV, AZ, HI	(415) 556-7747
Seattle	WA, OR, ID, AK	(206) 442-0229
Washington, DC	DC & Metrop. areas of VA, MD	(202) 472-7900

Help Protect Your Tax Dollars

Report *any* suspected instances of *fraud, waste, abuse or mismanagement* to the Inspector General Hotline:

- Operated 24 hours each day.
- All callers and writers may remain anonymous.
- Identities of all callers or writers are protected by Federal law.
- Regional callers or writers may contact any one of eleven (11) regional offices listed in this leaflet.
- To report suspected problems, please call or write:

HHS OIG HOTLINE
Post Office Box 17303
Department of Health & Human Services
Baltimore, Maryland 21203-7303
(301) 965-5953 (Commercial)

(FTS) 625-5953
(800) 368-5779 (Toll Free Nationwide)
(800) 638-3986 (Toll Free Maryland Only)

SPECIAL FRAUD ALERT: HOSPITAL INCENTIVES TO PHYSICIANS

The Office of Inspector General was established at the Department of Health and Human Services by Congress in 1976 to identify and eliminate fraud, abuse, and waste in Health and Human Services programs and to promote efficiency and economy in departmental operations. It carries out this mission through a nationwide network of audits, investigations, and inspections. To help reduce fraud in the Medicare and Medicaid programs, the Office of Inspector General is actively investigating violations of the Medicare and Medicaid antikickback statute, 42 U.S.C. § 1320a-7b(b). Among other things, the statute penalizes anyone who knowingly and willfully solicits, receives, offers, or pays remuneration in cash or in kind to induce, or in return for:

1. referring an individual to a person for the furnishing or arranging for the furnishing of any item or service payable under the Medicare or Medicaid program, or
2. purchasing, leasing, or ordering, or arranging for or recommending purchasing, leasing, or ordering any good, facility, service, or item payable under the Medicare or Medicaid programs.

Violations are subject to criminal penalties, or exclusion from participation in the Medicare and Medicaid programs, or both. In 1987, Section 14 of the Medicare and Medicaid Patient and Program Protection Act, P.L. 100-93, directed this Department to promulgate "safe harbor" regulations, in order to provide health care providers with a mechanism to assure them that they will not be prosecuted under the antikickback statute for engaging in particular practices. The Department published

---

Source: Reprinted from Department of Health & Human Services, Office of Inspector General, *Special Fraud Alert: Hospital Incentives to Physicians.*

final "safe harbor" regulations on July 29, 1991 (42 C.F.R. § 1001.952, 56 Fed. Reg. 35, 952). The scope of the antikickback statute is not expanded by the "safe harbor" regulations; these regulations given those in good faith compliance with a "safe harbor" the assurance that they will not be prosecuted under this statute.

Why Do Hospitals Provide Economic Incentives to Physicians?

As many hospitals have become more aggressive in their attempts to recruit and retain physicians and increase patient referrals, physician incentives (sometimess referred to as "practice enhancements") are becoming increasingly common. Some physicians actively solicit such incentives. These incentives may result in reductions in the physician's professional expenses or an increase in his or her revenues. In exchange, the physician is aware that he or she is often expected to refer the majority, if not all, of his or her patients to the hospital providing the incentives.

Why Is It Illegal For Hospitals To Provide Financial Incentives to Physicians For Their Referrals?

The Office of Inspector General has become aware of a variety of hospital incentive programs used to compensate physicians (directly or indirectly) for referring patients to the hospital. These arrangements are implicated by the antikickback statute because they can constitute remuneration offered to induce, or in return for, the referral of business paid for by Medicare or Medicaid. In addition, they are not protected under the existing "safe harbor" regulations.[2]

These incentive programs can interfere with the physician's judgment of what is the most appropriate care for a patient. They can inflate costs to the Medicare program by causing physicians to overuse inappropriately the services of a particular hospital. The incentives may result in the delivery of inappropriate care to Medicare beneficiaries and Medicaid recipients by inducing the physician to refer patients to the hospital providing financial incentives rather than to another hospital (or nonacute care facility) offering the best or most appropriate care for that patient.

Suspect Hospital Incentive Arrangement: What To Look For

To help identify suspect incentive arrangements, examples of practices that are often questionable are listed here. Please note that this list is not intended to be exhaustive but, rather, to suggest some indicators of potentially unlawful activity.

- Payment of any sort or incentive by the hospital each time a physician refers a patient to the hospital.
- The use of free or significantly discounted office space or equipment (in facilities usually located close to the hospital).
- Provision of free or significantly discounted billing, nursing, or other staff services.
- Free training for a physician's office staff in areas such as management techniques, CPT coding, and laboratory techniques.
- Guarantees that provide that, if the physician's income fails to reach a predetermined level, the hospital will supplement the remainder up to a certain amount.
- Low-interest or interest-free loans, or loans that may be "forgiven" if a physician refers patients (or some number of patients) to the hospital.
- Payment of the cost of a physician's travel and expenses for conferences.
- Payment for a physician's continuing education courses.
- Coverage on the hospital's group health insurance plans at an inappropriately low cost to the physician.
- Payment for services (which may include consultations at the hospital) that require few, if any, substantive duties by the physician, or payment for services in excess of the fair market value of services rendered.

Financial incentive packages that incorporate these or similar features may be subject to prosecution under the Medicare and Medicaid antikickback statute, if one of the purposes of the incentive is to influence the physician's medical decision as to where to refer his or her patients for treatment.

What To Do If You Have Information About Hospitals That Offer These Types of Incentives to Physicians

If you have information about hospitals that offer the types of incentives described above to physicians, contact any of the regional offices of the Office of Investigations of the Office of Inspector General, U.S. Department of Health and Human Services, at the following locations:

Regions	States Serviced	Telephone
Boston	MA, VT, NH, ME, RI, CT	(617) 565-2660
New York	NY, NJ, PR, VI	(212) 264-1691
Philadelphia	PA, MD, DE, WV, VA	(215) 596-6796
Atlanta	KY, GA, NC, SC, FL, TN, AL, MS	(404) 331-2131
Chicago	IL, MN, WI, MI, IN, OH	(312) 353-2740
Dallas	TX, NM, OK, AR, LA	(214) 767-8406
Kansas City	MO, KS	(816) 426-3811
Denver	CO, UT, WY, MT, ND, SD, IA, NE	(303) 844-5621
San Francisco	CA, NV, AZ, HI	(415) 556-8880
Seattle	WA, OR, ID, AK	(206) 553-0229
Washington, DC	DC & Metropolitan areas of VA, MD	(202) 619-1900

If there are special circumstances that make it inconvenient for you to contact one of the regional offices, you may report suspected violations to the Office of Inspector General Hotline, which is operated 24 hours each day. Written reports are preferred. Identities of all callers or writers are protected by federal law. The Office of Inspector General Hotline address and telephone numbers are:

HHS OIG HOTLINE
Department of Health & Human Services

Post Office Box 17303
Baltimore, Maryland 21203-7303
(301) 965-5953
625-5953 (FTS)
(800) 368-5779 (Toll Free Nationwide)

OIG MANAGEMENT ADVISORY REPORT: FINANCIAL ARRANGEMENTS BETWEEN HOSPITALS AND HOSPITAL-BASED PHYSICIANS

Date: January 31, 1991
From: Inspector General
Subject: OIG Management Advisory Report: "Financial Arrangements between Hospitals and Hospital-Based Physicians"
                OEI-09-89-0030
     To: Administrator
                Health Care Financing Administration

This management advisory report alerts you to potential violations of the antikickback statute (statute), Section 1128B of the Social Security Act (42 U.S.C. § 1320a-7b). We have identified potential violations in the financial arrangements between some hospitals and hospital-based physicians. These agreements (1) require physicians to pay more than the fair market value for services provided by the hospitals, or (2) compensate physicians for less than the fair market value of goods and services that they provide to hospitals.

Background

Hospital-based physicians include specialists such as anesthesiologists, emergency department physicians, pathologists, radiologists, and teaching physicians. Each of these specialties is dependent on the hospital environment to obtain referrals from other specialists practicing at the hospital. In turn, the

---

Source: Reprinted from Department of Health & Human Services, *Memorandum: OIG Management Advisory Report: "Financial Arrangements Between Hospitals and Hospital-Based Physicians."* OEI-09-89-0030, Jan. 31, 1991.

hospitals are somewhat dependent on the hospital-based physicians because they provide essential services to the hospitals.

Hospitals recently began to view these physicians as potential new revenue sources. Some hospitals have reduced payments to hospital-based physicians, and some are requiring payments from those physicians.

Medicare pays for the services of hospital-based physicians in a variety of ways. Usually, Medicare pays physicians directly for the services delivered. However, when pathologists perform clinical laboratory services for hospital inpatients under Part A, some portion of Medicare's payments to the hospital are for that pathology service. Different methods of payment may apply in each instance.

Medicare payments for anatomic pathology services are more complicated. Technical and professional components are paid separately. The former go directly to hospitals and the latter to the pathologist.

Legal Criteria

The statute makes it illegal to offer, pay, solicit, or receive remuneration for referring business payable under Medicare or Medicaid. Unlike most applications of the statute concerning Medicare compensation arrangements, the focus here is on remuneration made *to* hospitals.

The statute is very broad, covering indirect or covert forms of remuneration, bribes, kickbacks, and rebates as well as direct or overt ones. Three significant cases have interpreted the statute.

In *United States v. Greber,* 760 F.2d 68, 69 (3d Cir.), *cert. denied,* 474 U.S. 968 (1985), the Court held that, "if one purpose of the payment was to induce future referrals, the Medicare statute has been violated." The reasoning in *Greber* was adopted by the Ninth Circuit Court of Appeals in the *United States v. Kats,* 871 F.2d 105 (9th Cir. 1989). In *Kats* the Court found that the statute is violated unless the payments are "wholly and not incidentally attributable to the deliver of goods and services."

In *United States v. Lipkis,* 770 F.2d 1447 (1985), the Ninth Circuit Court of Appeals reviewed an arrangement between a medical management company that provided services to a physician's group and a clinical laboratory. The laboratory returned 20 percent of its revenues obtained from the physician group's referrals to the management company. The defendants alleged that these payments represented fair compensation for "specimen collection and handling services." The court rejected this defense, noting "the fair market value of these services was substantially less than the [amount paid], and there is no question [the laboratory] was paying for referrals as well as the described services." Thus, applying the reasoning of the Ninth Circuit Court of Appeals in *Lipkis,* an inference can be drawn that illegal remuneration occurs when a contract between hospital and hospital-based physicians calls for the rental of space or equipment or provision or professional services on terms other than fair market value.

If a provider's conduct falls within the purview of the statute, it can be prosecuted *unless* the conduct meets a statutory exception or "safe harbor" (when finalized). It should be observed that there is no statutory exception or contemplated "safe harbor" provision that applies to the conduct described herein.

Analysis

Contracts that require physicians to split portions of their income with hospitals are highly suspect, although not per se violations of the statute. Usually there is little basis to require hospital-based physicians to turn over a percentage of their earnings to the hospital. In addition, in many arrangements the fees hospitals receive are vastly in excess of the value of the services (such as billing services) they provide to the hospital-based physicians.

Examples of Agreements

We have reviewed many agreements that provide payments or remuneration to hospitals in excess of the fair market value of the services provided by them. Because many of these arrangements may violate the statute, disclosure of the terms of these agreements are rare, and therefore it is very difficult to establish the prevalence of these agreements. Several medical societies and anonymous parties have shown us the following contract provisions without identifying names and locations.

- A group of emergency department physicians pays a hospital half of its cash receipts exceeding $600,000 annually.
- A hospital provides no, or token, payback to pathologists for Part A services in return for the opportunity to perform Part B services at that hospital.
- Radiologists must pay 50 percent of their gross receipts to a facility's endowment fund.
- Thirty-three percent of all profits above a set amount must be paid by a radiology group to a hospital for its capital improvements, equipment, and other departmental expenditures.
- A radiologist group was required to purchase radiology equipment and agreed to donate the equipment to the hospital at the termination of the contract. The hospital has an unrestricted right to terminate the contract at any time.
- When net collections for a radiology group exceed $230,000, 50 percent is paid to the hospital, and the hospital reserves the right to unilaterally adjust the distributions if it determines that the physician group has not fulfilled the terms of the contract.
- A radiologist group pays 25 percent of the profits exceeding $120,000 to the hospital for capital improvements. Fifty percent of the profits exceeding $180,000 go to this purpose.
- A radiology group pays for facilities, services, supplies, personnel, utilities, maintenance, and billing services furnished by the hospital on a fee schedule that begins at $25,000 for 1989, and rises to $100,000 by 1993. Payments are due only if the radiologist's gross revenue exceeds $1 million in the previous year.

Conclusion

All of these examples appear to violate the statute because they provide compensation to the hospitals that exceeds the fair market value of the services the hospitals provide under the contracts. It also appears the payment of the remuneration is intended to provide the hospital-based physician with referrals from the other physicians on the hospital's medical staff.

These illegal financial arrangements may have several unfortunate results. The remuneration gives the hospitals a financial incentive to develop policies and practices that encourage greater utilization of the services of hospital-based physicians. Additionally, hospital-based physicians faced with lowered incomes may be encouraged to do more procedures in order to offset the payments to the hospitals. These problems are among the recognized purposes of having the antikickback statute on the books in the first place.

Illegal arrangements may also complicate the development of physician fee schedules if physician practice costs are artificially inflated by arrangements not based on fair market values.

Recommendation

The Health Care Financing Administration should instruct its contractors to: (1) notify physicians and hospitals about potential legal liability when they enter into agreements not based on the fair market value of necessary goods and services exchanged; and (2) refer identified cases to the Office of Inspector General for possible prosecution or sanctions.

To reduce potential legal liability, all contracts between hospitals and hospital-based physicians should be:

- Based on the fair market value of services (the nature and value of all services performed should be stated separately and the fair market value should be documented).
- Unrelated to physician income or billings (these agreements are not per se illegal but are suspect).
- Limited to goods and services necessary for the provision of medical services by the hospital-based physicians, and typical of what hospitals provide hospital-based physicians.

It should be noted explicitly that these criteria do *not* establish a "safe harbor." Compliance with these criteria will not immunize parties from liability under the statute.

SPECIAL FRAUD ALERT: PRESCRIPTION DRUG MARKETING SCHEMES

The Office of Inspector General (OIG) was established at the Department of Health and Human Services by Congress in 1976 to identify and eliminate fraud, abuse, and waste in Health and Human Services programs and to promote efficiency and economy in departmental operations. The OIG carries out this mission through a nationwide program of audits, investigations, and inspections. To help reduce fraud in the Medicare and Medicaid programs, the OIG is actively investigating violations of the Medicare and Medicaid antikickback statute, 42 U.S.C. § 1320a-7b(b).

What Is the Medicare and Medicaid Antikickback Law?

Among its provisions, the antikickback statute penalizes anyone who knowingly and willfully solicits, receives, offers, or pays remuneration in cash or in kind to induce or in return for:

1. referring an individual to a person for the furnishing, or arranging for the furnishing, of any item or service payable under the Medicare or Medicaid program; or
2. purchasing, leasing, or ordering, or arranging for or recommending purchasing, leasing, or ordering, any good, facility, service, or item payable under the Medicare or Medicaid program.

Violators are subject to criminal penalties, or exclusion from participation in the Medicare and Medicaid programs, or both. In 1987, Section 14 of the Medicare and Medicaid Patient and Program Protection Act, P.L. 100-93, directed this Department to promulgate "safe harbor" regulations in order to provide health care providers a mechanism to assure them that they will not be prosecuted under the antikickback statute for engaging in particular practices. The Department published 11 final "safe harbor" regulations on July 29, 1991 (42 C.F.R. §

Source: Reprinted from Department of Health & Human Services, Office of Inspector General, *Special Fraud Alert: Prescription Drug Marketing Schemes,* OIG-94-18 (Aug. 1994).

1001.952; 56 Fed. Reg. 35,952), and two more on November 5, 1992 (42 C.F.R. § 1001.952; 57 Fed. Reg. 52,723). The scope of the antikickback statute is not expanded by the "safe harbor" regulations; these regulations give those in good-faith compliance with a "safe harbor" the assurance that they will not be prosecuted under the antikickback statute.

How Does the Antikickback Law Relate to Prescription Drug Marketing Schemes?

In recent years, prescription drug companies in the United States have increased their marketing activities among providers, patients, and suppliers such as pharmacies. Many prescription drug marketing activities go far beyond traditional advertising and educational contacts. Physicians, suppliers, and, increasingly, patients are being offered valuable, nonmedical benefits in exchange for selecting specific prescription drug brands. Traditionally, physicians and pharmacists have been trusted to provide treatments and recommend products in the best interest of the patient. In an era of aggressive drug marketing, however, patients may now be using prescription drug items, unaware that their physician or pharmacist is being compensated for promoting the selection of a specific product. Prescription drugs supplied under one of these programs are often reimbursed under Medicaid. Among the specific activities, which the OIG has identified, are the following actual cases:

- A "product conversion" program that resulted in 96,000 brand-name conversions. In this scenario, for instance, Drug Company A offered a cash award to pharmacies for each time a drug prescription was changed from Drug Company B's product to Drug Company A's product. The pharmacies were induced to help persuade physicians, who were unaware of the pharmacies' financial interest, to change prescriptions.

- A "frequent flier" campaign in which physicians were given credit toward airline frequent flier mileage each time the physician completed a questionnaire for a new patient placed on the drug company's product.

- A "research grant" program in which physicians were given substantial payments for de minimis record-keeping tasks. The physician administered the drug manufacturer's product to the patient and made brief notes, sometimes a single word, about the treatment outcome. Upon completion of a limited number of such "studies," the physician received payment from the manufacturer.

If one purpose of any of these marketing schemes is to induce the provision of a prescription drug item reimbursable by Medicaid, then the criminal antikickback statute is implicated. There is no statutory exception or "safe harbor" to protect such activities. Thus, a physician, pharmacy, or other practitioner or supplier receiving payment under these activities may be subject to criminal prosecution and exclusion from participation in the Medicare and Medicaid programs.

A marketing program that is illegal under the antikickback statute may pose a danger to patients because the offering or percent of remuneration may interfere with a physician's judgment in determining the most appropriate treatment for a patient. Further, where the patient is a Medicaid beneficiary, these drug marketing practices may increase the federal government's costs of reimbursing suppliers for the products. The OIG is investigating various drug marketing schemes, and enforcing the antikickback laws where these practices affect the federal health care programs.

What To Look For

Generally, a payment or gift may be considered improper under 42 U.S.C. § 1320a-7b(b) if it is:

- Made to a person in a position to generate business for the paying party.
- Related to the volume of business generated.
- More than nominal in value and/or exceeds fair market value of any legitimate service rendered to the payer, or is unrelated to any service at all other than referral of patients.

OIG investigation may be warranted where one or more of the following features is present in prescription drug marketing activities:

- Any prize, gift, or cash payment; coupon or bonus (e.g., airline discounts and related travel premiums), offered to physicians and/or suppliers (including pharmacies, mail order prescription drug companies, and managed care organizations) in exchange for, or based on, prescribing or providing specific prescription products. These items are particularly suspect if based on value or volume of business generated for the drug company.

- Materials that offer cash or other benefits to pharmacists (or others in a position to recommend prescription drug products) in exchange for performing marketing tasks in the course of pharmacy practice related to Medicare or Medicaid. The marketing tasks may include sales-oriented "educational" or "counseling" contacts, or physician and/or patient outreach, etc.

- Grants to physicians and clinicians for studies of prescription products when the studies are of questionable scientific value and require little or no actual scientific pursuit. The grants may nonetheless offer substantial benefits based on, or related to, use of the product.

- Any payment, including cash or other benefit, given to a patient, provider, or supplier for changing a prescription, or recommending or requesting such a change, from one product to another, unless the payment is made fully consistent with a "safe harbor" regulation, 42 C.F.R. § 1001.952, or other federal provision governing the reporting of prescription drug prices.

What To Do If You Have Information About Suspect Prescription Drug Marketing Activities

If you have information about drug companies or other providers engaging in the types of activities described above, contact any of the regional offices or the office of Investigations of the Office of Inspector General, U.S. Department of Health and Human Services, at the following locations:

Regions	States Serviced	Telephone
Boston	MA, VT, NH, ME, RI, CT	617-565-2660
New York	NY, NJ, PR, VI	212-264-1691
Philadelphia	PA, MD, DE, WV, VA	215-596-6796
Atlanta	GA, KY, NC, SC, FL, TN, AL, MS (No. District)	404-331-2131
Chicago	IL, MN, WI, MI, IN, OH, IA, MO (So. District)	312-353-2740
Dallas	TX, NM, OK, AR, LA, MO	214-767-8406
Denver	CO, UT, WY, MT, ND, SD, NE, KS	303-844-5621
Los Angeles	AZ, NV (Clark Co.), So. CA	714-836-2372
San Francisco	No. CA, NV, AZ, HI, OR, ID, WA	415-556-8880
Washington, DC	DC & Metropolitan areas of VA & MD	202-619-1900

SPECIAL FRAUD ALERT: ARRANGEMENTS FOR THE PROVISION OF CLINICAL LAB SERVICES

The Office of Inspector General (OIG) was established at the Department of Health and Human Services by Congress in 1976 to identify and eliminate fraud, abuse, and waste in Departmental programs and to promote efficiency and economy in their operations. The OIG carries out this mission through a nationwide program of audits, investigations, and inspections. To help reduce fraud in the Medicare and Medicaid programs, the OIG is actively investigating violations of the Medicare and Medicaid antikickback statute, 42 U.S.C. § 1320a-7b(b).

What Is the Medicare and Medicaid Antikickback Law?

Among its provisions, the antikickback statute penalizes anyone who knowingly and willfully solicits, receives, offers, or pays remuneration in cash or in kind to induce or in return for:

1. referring an individual to a person or entity of the furnishing, or arranging for the furnishing, of any item or service payable under the Medicare or Medicaid program, or

---

Source: Reprinted from Department of Health & Human Services, Office of Inspector General, *Special Fraud Alert: Arrangements for the Provision of Clinical Lab Services*, OIG-95-03 (Oct. 1994).

2. purchasing, leasing or ordering, or arranging for or recommending purchasing, leasing, or ordering any good, facility, service, or item payable under the Medicare or Medicaid programs.

Violators are subject to criminal penalties, or exclusion from participation in the Medicare and Medicaid programs, or both. In 1987, Section 14 of the Medicare and Medicaid Patient and Program Protection Act, P.L. 100-93, directed this Department to promulgate "safe harbor" regulations in order to provide health care providers a mechanism to assure them that they will not be prosecuted under the antikickback statute for engaging in particular practices. The Department published 11 final "safe harbor" regulations on July 29, 1991 (42 C.F.R. § 1001.952; 56 Fed. Reg. 35,952), and two more on November 5, 1992 (42 C.F.R. § 1001.952; 57 Fed. Reg. 52,723). The scope of the antikickback statute is not expanded by the "safe harbor" regulations; these regulations give those in good-faith compliance with a "safe harbor" the assurance that they will not be prosecuted under the antikickback statute.

How Does the Antikickback Statute Relate to Arrangements For the Provision of Clinical Lab Services?

Many physicians and other health care providers rely on the services of outside clinical laboratories to which they may refer high volumes of patient specimens every day. The quantity, timeliness, and cost of these services are of obvious concern to Medicare and Medicaid patients and to the programs that finance their health care services. Since the physician, not the patient, generally selects the clinical laboratory, it is essential that the physician's decision regarding where to refer specimens is based only on the best interests of the patient.

Whenever a laboratory offers or gives to a source of referrals anything of value not paid for at fair market value, the inference may be made that the thing of value is offered to induce the referral of business. The same is true whenever a referral source solicits or receives anything of value from the laboratory.

By "fair market value" we mean value for general commercial purposes. However, "fair market value" must reflect an arms length transaction that has not been adjusted to include the additional value that one or both of the parties has attributed to the referral of business between them.

The Office of Inspector General has become aware of a number of practices engaged in by clinical laboratories and health care providers that implicate the antikickback statute in this manner. Below are some examples of lab services arrangements that may violate the antikickback statute.

Provision of Phlebotomy Services to Physicians

Where permitted by State law, a laboratory may make available to a physician's office a phlebotomist who collects specimens from patients for testing by the outside laboratory. While the mere placement of a laboratory employee in the physician's office would not necessarily serve as an inducement prohibited by the antikickback statute, the statute is implicated when the phlebotomist performs additional tasks that are normally the responsibility of the physician's office staff. These tasks can include taking vital signs or other nursing functions, testing for the physician's office laboratory, or performing clerical services.

Where the phlebotomist performs clerical or medical functions not directly related to the collection or processing of laboratory specimens, a strong inference arises that he or she is providing a benefit in return for the physician's referrals to the laboratory. In such a case, the physician, the phlebotomist, and the laboratory may have exposure under the antikickback statute. This analysis applies equally to the placement of phlebotomists in other health care settings, including nursing homes, clinics, and hospitals.

Further, the mere existence of a contract between the laboratory and the health care provider that prohibits the phlebotomist from performing services unrelated to specimen collection does not eliminate the OIG's concern, where the phlebotomist is not closely monitored by his employer or where the contractual prohibition is not rigorously enforced.

Lab Pricing at Renal Dialysis Centers

The Medicare program pays for laboratory tests provided to patients with end stage renal disease (ESRD) in two different ways. Some laboratory testing is considered routine and payment is included in the composite rate paid by Medicare to the ESRD facility, which in turn pays the laboratory. Some laboratory testing required by the patient is not included in the composite rate, and these additional tests are billed by the laboratory directly to Medicare and paid at the usual laboratory fee schedule price.

The OIG is aware of cases where a laboratory offers to perform the tests encompassed by the composite rate at a price below the fair market value of the tests performed. In order to offset the low charges on the composite rate tests, the ESRD facility agrees to refer all or most of its noncomposite rate tests to the laboratory. This arrangement appears to be an offer of something of value (composite rate tests at below fair market value) in return for the ordering of additional tests that are billed directly to the Medicare program.

If offered or accepted in return for referral or additional business, the lab's pricing scheme is illegal remuneration under the antikickback statute. The statutory exception and "safe harbor" for "discounts" does not apply to immunize parties to this type of transaction, since discounts on the composite rate tests are offered to induce referral of *other* tests. See 42 C.F.R. § 1001.952(h)(3)(ii).

Waiver of Charges to Managed Care Patients

Managed care plans may require a physician or other health care provider to use only the laboratory with which the plan has negotiated a fee schedule. In such situations, the plan usually will refuse to pay claims submitted by other laboratories. The provider, however, may use a different laboratory and may wish to continue to use that laboratory for nonmanaged care patients. In order to retain the provider as a client, the laboratory that does not have the managed care contract may agree to perform the managed care work free of charge.

The status of such agreements under the antikickback statute depends in part on the nature of the contractual relationship between the managed care plan and its providers. Under the terms of many managed care contracts, a provider receives a bonus or other payment if utilization of ancillary services, such as laboratory testing, is kept below a particular level. Other managed care plans impose financial penalties if the provider's utilization of services exceeds pre-established levels. When the laboratory agrees to write off charges for the physician's managed care work, the physician may realize a financial benefit from the managed care plan created by the appearance that utilization of tests has been reduced.

In cases where the provision of free services results in a benefit to the provider, the antikickback statute is implicated. If offered or accepted in return for the referral of Medicare or State health care plan business, both the laboratory and the physician may be violating the antikickback statute. There is no statutory exception or "safe harbor" to immunize any party to such a practice because the federal programs do not realize the benefit of these "free" services. *See* 42 C.F.R. § 1001.952(h)(3) (iii).

Other Inducements

The following are additional examples of inducements offered by clinical laboratories that may implicate the antikickback statute:

- Free pick-up and disposal of biohazardous waste products (such as sharps) unrelated to the collection of specimens for the outside laboratory.
- Provision of computers or fax machines, unless such equipment is integral to, and exclusively used for, performance of the outside laboratory's work.
- Provision of free laboratory testing for health care providers, their families, and their employees.

Where one purpose of these arrangements is to induce the referral of program-reimbursed laboratory testing, both the clinical laboratory and the health care provider may be liable under the statute and may be subject to criminal prosecution and exclusion from participation in the Medicare and Medicaid programs.

What To Do If You Have Information About Suspect Clinical Laboratory Arrangements

If you have information about laboratories, physicians, or health care providers engaging in the types of activities described above, contact any of the regional offices of the Office of Investigations of the Office of Inspector General, U.S. Department of Health and Human Services, at the following locations:

Regions	States Serviced	Telephone
Boston	MA, VT, NH, ME, RI, CT	617-565-2660
New York	NY, NJ, PR, VI	212-264-1691
Philadelphia	PA, MD, DE, WV, VA	215-596-6796
Atlanta	GA, KY, NC, SC, FL, TN, AL, MS (No. District)	404-331-2131
Chicago	IL, MN, WI, MI, IN, OH, IA, MO	312-353-2740
Dallas	TX, NM, OK, AR, LA, MS (So. District)	214-767-8406
Denver	CO, UT, WY, MT, ND, SD, NE, KS	303-844-5621
Los Angeles	AZ, NV (Clark Co.), So. CA	714-836-2372
San Francisco	No. CA, NV, AZ, HI, OR, ID, WA	415-556-8880
Washington, DC	DC & Metropolitan areas of VA & MD	202-619-1900

MEDICARE FRAUD ALERT: Fraud Alert OIG 97-01

An investigation into laboratory billing irregularities in several Ohio hospitals has shown that the practice of fragmenting lab billings was promoted by consulting firms that promised to increase hospital revenue in return for a commission consisting of a percentage of the first year's increase. The department heads of several hospitals were interviewed for insight into the decision making process which resulted in the submission of false laboratory claims by hospitals. When interviewed, technical and financial supervisors of Ohio hospitals indicated that there are a number of consulting firms which offer to maximize billings for radiology, emergency room, and laboratory services by discovering and correcting coding "errors" in return for a percentage of the resulting revenue increase.

There is little incentive for consultants to correct coding errors which do not increase their consulting fees. This arrangement is ripe for upcoding, unbundling, and other manipulation which increases costs to the Medicare program. However, hospital business managers tend to rely heavily on representations made by the consultant, and fixing responsibility in a hospital organization can be difficult. Organizational charts, reporting relationships and lines of authority can and should be explored and documented in personal interviews with hospital officials. These can be essential elements in developing a criminal case.

It is recommended that OIG Special Agents become aware of the implications of this consulting practice. Special Agents performing cost report investigations or investigating other hospital practices should take steps to determine whether there are such contracts in effect and make note of them. Contact should be made with fiscal intermediaries for the purpose of developing patterns by comparing groups of consultant customers to other selected hospitals.

NOTES

1. This fraud alert is not intended to address the routine waiver of copayments and deductibles by providers, practitioners, or suppliers who are paid on the basis of costs or diagnostic related groups. The fact that these types of services are not discussed in this fraud alert should not be interpreted to legitimize routine waiver of deductibles and copayments with respect to these payment methods. Also, it does not apply to a waiver of any copayment by a federally qualified health care center with respect to an individual who qualifies for subsidized services under a provision of the *Public Health Service Act*.

2. The Department is considering seeking public comment on the advisability of granting protection under the "safe harbor" regulations for certain hospital incentives for physicians starting a new practice. However, such a concept would have no legal effect whatsoever until promulgated as a final regulation.

Index